The Soldier's Story

THE AMERICAN CIVIL WAR

The Soldier's Story

THE AMERICAN CIVIL WAR

Hans Halberstadt

Brassey's, Inc.

Washington, D.C.

DEDICATION

For Jon and Stu, the Confederates in our family attic.

ACKNOWLEDGMENTS

Well, I hardly know who to blame first, so many people have helped with this project in so many ways. It is amazing that, more than 135 years after the conclusion of the military festivities, there remains such fascination, passion, and scholarship about the American Civil War, particularly in an era when our culture seems to look forward at the newest technology and almost never over its shoulder at the past. This is – for those of us with any link to it at all – a fight between members of our great-great-grandfathers' generation; according to conventional wisdom, we shouldn't care about it at all, and yet we do, all these years later.

I am indebted to the scholarship and generosity of each of the following for their assistance with this work. Occasionally, their scholarship and mine have come up with conflicting answers to questions and puzzles, the resolution of which is one of the charms of the study of Civil War history.

Jerry Decius, 1st Company, Battalion of Sharpshooters, McGowan's Brigade of South Carolinians; Phillip Bolte, BG USA (Ret.), President, US Cavalry Association; Ruben Chavez, Richie Figueroa, Clinton Pautsch, John McIntire; Loren Griffin, an old, combat soldier who knows all there is to know about artillery, past and present; LTC Shardon Lewis, and Capt. Linneas Ahearn, both of the 9th Virginia Cavalry, for their guidance on Civil War cavalry; Trooper Edwin Sims, US Cavalry Association, for guidance on Union cav weapons, tack, and doctrine; Michael Fostar, President, National Civil War Association, for his help and hospitality before and during battle; Ted Stahr, for his excellent scholarship on all sorts of issues, particularly Federal weapons; RJ Samp, who knows more about Civil War bugling than most Civil War buglers did; and to Capt. Rick Barrum of the 72nd New York Infantry, 5th Texas Infantry, 9th Virginia Cavalry, 34th North Carolina Infantry, 1st Company, Battalion of Sharpshooters, South Carolina Volunteers, and their latter-day ghosts, for many kindnesses and considerations.

Contents

Preface

I've been studying soldiering and soldiers for 40 years now, since I became a soldier myself at the now-distant age of 18. That was back in the days of the draft, when all kinds of men served in uniform, and, coincidentally, a period of service that was a century after the Civil War.

My service was as a common soldier in another nation's civil war, a member of the rank and file rather than an officer. As a volunteer, I was proud to be a regular rather than a draftee – back when the Army made such distinctions. Part of my service was in Virginia, Georgia, and Alabama, and I served alongside men from those states, men whose ancestors wore gray and "butternut," and who were loyal to both the Confederacy and the post-Civil War Union at the same time. The Civil War – or the War of Northern Aggression, if you prefer – was a living memory then and there, as it still is today, 135 years and more after the guns fell silent.

There are a lot of books about the Civil War – too many, perhaps – but I thought there was a need for one more. The existing books mostly celebrate the leaders – Lee, Grant, Stuart, Sheridan, and their lieutenants. As important as the roles of these combat leaders may have been, however, few of them ever pulled a trigger on an enemy, spending much of their time in comparative safety and (for most, but not all) comparative comfort.

The common soldier, on the other hand, outnumbers these famous senior commanders about a hundred thousand to one, yet we don't hear as much as we might about their military skills, their fieldcraft, and their lives in and out of the line.

Now, I like officers well enough – some of my best friends are Army officers – but they are not always as important to a battle as some may believe, particularly while the guns are firing.

Officers' work, and particularly general officers' work, is seeing the big picture and preparing for the battle – the administrative details, the overall plan, the logistics, and coordination. An officer's most important aspect of leadership is brought into play before the battle, insuring that everybody is –

as we say today – "playing off the same sheet of music," and nothing he may do on the battlefield will redeem his failures before the fight.

Sergeants' work involves preparation, too, but is much farther out on the pointy end of the spear, controlling and maneuvering the squads and fire teams, pulling the triggers, aiming the cannon, swinging the saber – closing with and destroying the enemy. A sergeant kills people, face to face; an officer generally tells other people to do his killing for him. Both roles, we all know, are essential to the business, but we hear an awful lot about the officer's story and not so much about the private's and sergeant's.

And besides that, there is a common misconception that soldiers automatically respect officers and officers' guidance; new second lieutenants, if they know anything at all, know better. Among the many insulting and demeaning things a young officer will hear during his career, nothing exceeds the subtle implications that can be worked into the expression "Yes, sir," spoken by an old professional combat soldier with a few stripes on his sleeve, a delivery that can clearly mean "Are you out of your Goddamned mind?" to everybody within hearing.

Officers of any era receive a certain level of superficial respect because of the "butter bar" or other insignia on their jackets, but a deeper level of trust and respect must be earned by proven performance, particularly in time of war. Soldiers and their officers have always had a kind of adversarial labor-management relationship, and that was as true during the Civil War as it is today, perhaps more so.

Since my affection and allegiance is to the troops, the sergeants, and the junior officers who actually led soldiers in battle – the working-class, blue- and gray-collar men of the Civil War, who did the dirty work, Unionized or not – this book is primarily about them and their experiences in America's most interesting war, with just a few references to the senior officers to keep them from getting too mad at me (again).

I make one small exception in the form of Brigadier Henry M. Naglee, who is so much a part of my family that I

couldn't write such a book and leave him out. I live on his old estate, his great-granddaughter is a friend, and my wife is infatuated with him to the point where, if he was still alive, I would have to kill him. Naglee was a "ring-knocker" from West Point (Class of '35), a professional, and a man who wrote the best love letters – of a certain gooey type – of anybody in the whole war. If nothing else, Naglee's letters illustrate the state of mind of the commanders whom the soldiers and sergeants had to follow.

The American Civil War is such a broad, deep, intensely emotional story that thousands of books have been written about its broad sweep and obscure details. And there is a vast host of scholars, students, authors, and experts who all claim to have a special insight concerning one aspect of the conflict or another. A major problem with a book like this is not coming up with good material, it is sorting out the conflicting claims of people who think they know for sure what happened before any of us were born. Any critics are invited to contact the author at hans@militaryphoto.com – and the first punch, as always, is free.

Hans Halberstadt
October 2000

RIGHT *Etching of a Union soldier: in fact the infantry enlisted man's belt plate was oval, made of brass backed with lead and between January 1861 and June 1866 the Army bought 143,348 of them.*

Reenactment

Today, it is said, more people refight Gettysburg each year than took part in the original battle. All over the United States — and even in Europe — fascination in the Civil War has led people to faithfully recreate the uniforms, units, and battles that took place between 1861 and 1865. They do so in great detail, with particular emphasis on verisimilitude, and with a great awareness of history.

For the photographer, this presents a wonderful opportunity to provide images that do not exist from the past: color photographs of events and actions that happened nearly 150 years ago. For the author, it allows production of a book such as this one — a colorful evocation of what it was like to live and fight through the Civil War using new material, rather than the black and white photographs that, because they are relatively few in number, have been seen so often.

In the 1860s photography was still a relatively new science, and war photographers few and far between. The work of pioneers such as Mathew B. Brady provide us with a wonderful record of the war, but little of the color and action an audience today is used to seeing.

The "Soldier's Story" series is designed to provide readers with a different view of the world's battlefields, and one of the ways it accomplishes this is through the use of reenactment photographs. There are certainly some drawbacks: the "soldiers" tend to be healthier — certainly fatter! — and there are the occasional problems with wristwatches and sunglasses. In the main, however, just as a good movie can take the viewer back in time, so can these photographs. They have been captioned as if they were "live action," but I can report that the casualties were few, all living to fight another day.

LEFT *Confederate infantry in the Army of Northern Virginia muster under the colors of the Commonwealth of Virginia at the Battle of Cedar Mountain, Virginia.*

ABOVE *Confederate soldiers begin to break ranks as they lunge toward the Union line, giving their famous "Rebel Yell" as they closed on their enemy.*

The Call to Arms

There were three kinds of Union soldier and soldiering organization at the beginning of the war – militia, volunteer, and regular – each with its own traditions, procedures, and character. Soldiers in one kind of regiment tended to have strong opinions about men in the others, seldom flattering.

REGULARS

The then-tiny US Army fought an extremely successful war against Mexico between 1846 and 1848. Although some volunteer regiments were organized for that war, the fighting was done by the regulars, the full-time professionals. Among this little band of brothers were the first graduates of West Point, many of whom used their classroom training against the Mexicans with great effectiveness.

After the war with Mexico, the US Army remained fairly small, with about 16,000 officers and soldiers, but developed competence and confidence that were based on results in the real world. It was a professional force, officer and enlisted, that went on to fight the Indians across the developing west, patrolling the vast new territory acquired from Mexico.

These pre-Civil War operations against the Indians required a new kind of military thinking and a new kind of cavalry, contrary to the popular doctrine of the day, based as it was on the European model and the experience of the Napoleonic wars.

About 40 percent of the Regular officer corps came from the Southern states, and when those states seceded, half of the Southern West Pointers and all but one of the Southern officers who acquired their commissions in other ways quit the US Army for that of the Confederacy.

Enlisted regular soldiers and non-commissioned officers (NCOs) were far more loyal at the outbreak of war. Very few quit the US Army for the Confederacy. Regardless of where their loyalties lay, these professional soldiers formed the hardcore of both sides' military organizations.

A Federal regular enlisted or, after 1864, was drafted into a regiment sponsored by the Federal government – like the 1st US Cavalry or the 19th US Infantry – at a recruiting office operated by the Federal government, not his local state. He received his pay and uniform from a different personnel system than did the volunteers and militia. Regulars had a reputation for steadiness under fire and for professionalism. They came from all over the Union, unlike the militia and state volunteers, giving their regiments a rather more cosmopolitan character than other units. In contrast to the other kinds of regiment, the officers and NCOs of the regulars were appointed rather than elected – they didn't have to participate in a popularity contest as did the others.

MILITIAS

Then there were the state militias. Well over three million men enrolled in state militias in 1860, with 650,000 in the southern states. At the time, fewer than four percent (115,000) had any real training or equipment.

RIGHT *Boys as young as 12 managed to enlist in both armies, sometimes as drummers and sometimes as riflemen.*
BELOW *The residue of Company D, 149th Pennsylvania Infantry – 35 men out of the original 100 – pose for their portrait in November 1864.*

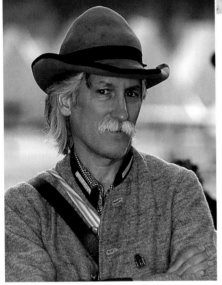

ABOVE *Company G, 114th Pennsylvania Infantry at Petersburg, Virginia, August 1864, still wearing their Zouave uniforms.*
LEFT *Older men enlisted, too, but few over 40 could stand the rigors of active campaigning.*
RIGHT *Will Lynn, a sailor with the Confederate Navy, tied a black flag to his saber. The meaning: "I take no quarter. I take no prisoners."*

Prior to the war, the militias were essentially social organizations with very little practical military function. They put more money and effort into their custom-tailored, and often unique, uniforms than into practical military operations. They could do parade-ground drill with the precision of a high-school marching band, and they looked terrific at a parade or a fancy-dress ball, but few of their members – North or South – had joined with the expectation of ever becoming involved in a real shooting war.

But things heated up gradually for years before the war, and in the South, the militias and volunteer military organizations took the possibility of war much more seriously than those in the North. They bought weapons and trained with them, particularly after about 1860, and began to prepare to fight.

By late 1860, and with Lincoln's election, when war began to seem likely, Northern militia units suddenly started to lose officers and men who liked soldiering well enough, just as long as it didn't involve bloodshed. Papers published their names and portraits, and they became outcasts for a while.

President Lincoln called them up after Fort Sumter was fired on in April 1861, for 90 days, primarily to defend Washington from possible attack. The only real fighting most of them had to cope with was getting through the city of Baltimore, where Confederate sympathies were strong and active. But those 90 days were a learning experience.

VOLUNTEERS

Most of the soldiers, North and South, went to war with volunteer state regiments – the 9th Pennsylvania Cavalry, for example, or the 1st Georgia Infantry. These organizations employed men from one state, often from one town or city, who had often been acquainted before the war. Volunteer regiments were typically recruited by local men of accomplishment and standing in the community – successful businessmen or farmers or politicians – and many of them had no

trouble in getting a thousand of their friends and neighbors to sign up. Their reward for this recruiting duty was command of the unit, often despite a lack of any military experience or aptitude.

Officers and NCOs in volunteer regiments were elected, not appointed, from the top down. Popularity contests are not a good way to select combat leaders, men who sometimes must make life-or-death decisions about subordinates, and there were tremendous problems with these volunteer regiments in the early months of the war. Those problems were largely resolved by tightening up the system of command, and a lot of those elected officers were weeded out early on. While the volunteer regiments had a reputation for being less disciplined than the regulars, some were as good as any on the battlefield – the legendary Iron Brigade, the 1st Vermont, Hood's Texas Brigade (Confederate) among many others.

Dressed for War

ABOVE, RIGHT *Sergeant R. W. Bowles, well scrubbed, shaved, and oiled, sits for his portrait. He wears his ceremonial sword and sash of office.*

Civil War planners relied heavily on European models for much of their tactics and uniforms, both of which were a little out of place in the dis-United States. The French, Germans, Russians, and British had been sparring with each other on the European mainland off and on for many years prior to 1861, and had evolved their own traditions and techniques for bloodletting.

The French, in particular, refused to go to war unless it was combined with a kind of large-scale fashion show with guns and knives. They insisted on extremely elaborate, gaudy, and generally worthless items of personal equipment for both rank-and-file and officers – feather plumes, hats, uncomfortable uniforms, and equipment that was difficult to carry and inefficient in use – but that looked simply smashing!

THE ZOUAVES

Among the most gaudily attired Civil War soldiers were the Zouaves, who wore red baggy uniforms, complete with a very silly little fez – also in red – in a fashion statement that virtually said, "Shoot me, please." Even so, the French Army had superb light infantry units wearing these uniforms, and Captain George McClellan, who had seen the French Zouaves in action while an observer in the Crimea and had sent reports back to American newspapers, popularized them in the years before the war.

Elmer Ellsworth raised a company of militia about this time, the Chicago Zouave Cadets. They were really no more than a glorified drill team, but they were very good and very flashy. Ellsworth's Zouave Cadets dominated the drill competitions that were as popular in the pre-Civil War years as basketball is today. They drew huge crowds and extensive press coverage; their novel uniforms with bright red baggy trousers, combined with the precision drill performance, created a sensation.

As the threat of war increased, Ellsworth started recruiting among New York firemen, a notoriously tough and disciplined gang at the time, and raised his own new Zouave regiment. Known at first as the 1st New York Fire Zouaves (later the 11th New York Volunteers), the regiment marched off to war only two weeks after the bombardment of Fort Sumter.

There was a kind of Zouave frenzy among many new regiments, partly as a result of the fame of Ellsworth's Zouave Cadets, and partly from the fame gained by the French light infantry in the Crimea and North Africa. Some units (North and South) adopted the Zouave uniform, complete with the fez, and were still wearing it into battle at the beginning of the war. The 5th New York Volunteer Infantry – formed just before the assault on Fort Sumter – wore the Zouave outfit through the war. They attained a superb record for valor and sacrifice, although the Confederate riflemen cut their ranks to shreds.

During the course of the war, the bright uniform of the Zouaves became the mark of a particularly brave and exemplary soldier. Zouaves were willing to tempt fate, didn't give a damn, and notoriously were ready to lead the assault. They were superb in close-order drill and highly disciplined in combat. Their war cry was "ZOOOOZS!" and it could be heard over the roar of the traditional Union "HURRAH!" in battle.

The cult of the Zouave continued throughout the war, and at one time more than 50 regiments wore a Zouave outfit.

By the end, about ten percent of Federal troops wore some variant of the uniform, and all were considered elite troops, on and off the battlefield. Most were Union organizations, though; Rebel regiments gave up the uniform early, except for the Louisiana Tigers. The last Federal soldier killed before General Robert E. Lee surrendered the Army of Northern Virginia wore the Zouave uniform of the 155th Pennsylvania.

But the Zouaves weren't the only ones in the military fashion show; there was the 79th New York Cameron Highlanders Regiment, who marched off to war in 1861 wearing traditional Scottish uniforms – doublets, glengarry bonnets, and kilts. The Highlanders had the good sense to send the kilts home, however, before the serious fighting began for them on July 21, 1861, at the first Battle of Bull Run.

CONFEDERATE UNIFORMS

The uniform of the Rebel soldier varied tremendously, from marvelously tailored elegance to rag-tag shreds of homespun and bare feet. Some of the Confederate states, including Georgia, Virginia, Maryland, and the Carolinas, managed to provide their soldiers with good-quality manufactured uniforms from well-stocked depots. These uniforms were of virtually identical pattern to those of the Union, with minor variations of color and detail. The Army of Northern Virginia kept its soldiers pretty well supplied with regulation gray uniforms right up till the last year of the war.

Officially, the common Confederate soldier was supposed to wear a long (to mid-thigh) coat with two rows of buttons and a stand-up collar, in a color called "cadet gray," which was based on the color of the uniform of West Point cadets. The collar and sleeves were expected to be trimmed with material indicating branch of service – blue for infantry, red for artillery, and yellow for cavalry.

But many Confederate soldiers, particularly in the western theater, were in the volunteer militia tradition of the first American Revolution, particularly at the outset of the war, and brought their own uniforms from home. For these troops, there wasn't much uniform about any of them. Their clothing was often

ABOVE, LEFT *Private Mark G. Edwards and Sergeant Emery Hamlin of the 4th US Colored Troops at duty stations.*
LEFT *First Sergeant Stephen R. Bockmiller, US Marine Corps assigned to the USS Constellation (circa 1859–68).*
RIGHT *Captain Daley and Sergeant Barry Kluck of the 5th New York Regiment, the Zouaves, review assignments at the site of an old grain mill.*

made of homespun cloth, cut and stitched by hand by a wife, mother, or sister.

Their coats and pants were whatever they could come up with, and if they couldn't acquire home-made, these Rebel soldiers often captured or scavenged clothing from Union forces. Although wearing such items of attire unmodified put them at risk of being shot or captured and even execution, many wore them anyway. There was nothing else.

Union-blue jackets and pants were often dyed as black as walnut shells would make them in an effort to differentiate them and their wearer as belonging to the Confederacy. Even so, there was much confusion on the battlefield regarding the true identity of units – Federal cavalry (like the 7th Ohio on an 1862 raid in Tennessee) sometimes pretended to be Rebels, and got away with it.

Home manufacture of clothing was very common in the South at the time, but there wasn't any practical way to dye homespun cotton cloth the regulation "cadet gray" color. Instead, those wives, sisters, and mothers used walnut shells and copperas to produce a kind of creamy tan shade called "butternut." However, a Confederate soldier's coat and pants were likely to be any shade of very light blue, brown, tan, yellow, or even rarely "cadet gray."

For headgear, the Rebel soldier very sensibly preferred a light straw farmer's hat in summer, or perhaps a broad-brimmed felt hat for year-round wear. The Confederate regulations also indicated that the soldier should wear a forage cap with a short leather bill and flat top, essentially the same as that worn by Union soldiers.

Soldiers of both sides were supposed to receive one pair of sturdy shoes, two sets of underwear, a shirt, jacket, greatcoat, and socks. The Federal troops generally obtained theirs through the normal channels of supply, complete, then threw many of the items away on the march.

The Rebels got theirs from the Federal supply system by picking up whatever they needed where the Union soldiers had thrown it. The route of march was littered with such items, while the line of retreat added weapons and accessories. In fact, a great many Confederate soldiers carried Union haversacks, muskets, bayonets, knapsacks, canteens, and cartridge boxes. A lot of them didn't care and wore the items anyway, just the way they were, till they fell apart from long use.

LOAD-BEARING EQUIPMENT

Nobody goes off to war without a minimum of about 30 pounds of gear – typically weapons, ammunition, and water – and the basic combat load of a modern soldier is just about the same as it was for the troops a 1,000 years ago. That weight is easily calculated – just as much as a normal man can reasonably carry, plus ten pounds. During the Civil War, trussed up like a Christmas turkey, that was about 60 pounds including weapon.

For the common infantry soldier on campaign, the load included a belt on which were mounted the bayonet scabbard, cartridge box with 40 rounds, and small leather box for the musket's percussion caps. Cavalry soldiers needed two cartridge boxes, one for the carbine and another for the pistol.

Artillery crews didn't have muskets, so dispensed with the cartridge boxes, but some carried short swords on their belts, while others had pistols.

A strap over his right shoulder supported the soldier's haversack, carried on the left hip. When a Federal soldier was just departing on campaign, this bag would be stuffed with rations for at least three days – that means about two-and-a-half pounds of salt pork, three pounds of hardtack, plus coffee beans, sugar, and other items of the soldier's personal selection. In addition, the haversack would contain his grimy tin plate, while on the outside, with the strap running through the cup handle, was a blackened tin cup that usually doubled as a coffee pot.

The Confederate soldier had a similar rig, but more likely than not, his haversack would have been loaded with corn pone instead of hardtack, and been devoid of coffee and sugar unless those rare commodities had been captured recently.

All carried some sort of canteen, also over the right shoulder, extending to the left hip. Those of the Federals were made of tin, the Confederates using wooden versions till they could pick up Federal canteens on the road or battlefield.

At the beginning of the war, soldiers on both sides were certain to carry a knapsack of fashionable French design, reinforced with thin wooden boards and uncomfortable as hell. In the knapsack, the soldier was supposed to carry his spare clothing, extra ammunition, personal items (Bible, letters, writing materials, soap, candle, matches), and sometimes additional food besides that

LEFT *A grimy private from the 34th North Carolina Infantry in light marching order.* BELOW *Civil War soldiers regularly wore their uniforms until they fell apart, as shown by the jacket of this Confederate sergeant from the 5th Texas Infantry.* BOTTOM *Officers and NCOs pose for their portrait in a mixed bag of un-uniform coats, hats, and footgear.*

already in the haversack. On the outside was strapped the soldier's blanket, greatcoat, tent half, and rubber ground sheet. The rigid knapsack was replaced about 1862 with an unreinforced version, the infamous soft pack, which had its own problems: straps across the soldier's chest restricted breathing, but it was more comfortable than its predecessor.

The outside of the knapsack was frequently stenciled or painted with the name of the regiment and the soldier to which it belonged. This facilitated finding the proper item after a battle, since the soldiers typically were ordered to cache their gear at a rally point well away from the expected battlefield. But many of these Federal caches were abandoned during the first few years of the war, the piles of knapsacks then being scavenged by the victorious Confederates, who later

might be seen on the march wearing equipment marked "14th Brooklyn" or with some similar proud label.

Stuffed to the gills, the knapsack weighed about 45 pounds. That wouldn't have been a bad load, except that its design put the weight on the shoulders and lower back in a painful way, and without permitting much ventilation for the soldier's skin on those hot, humid hikes under the southern sun.

So the soldiers quickly learned to adopt a fairly extreme version of "light marching order." They started down the road toward their first campaign with all their issued items intact, but began shedding them within the first mile. On really hot days, the blankets and greatcoat were discarded right away. The contents of the knapsack went next, in order of importance. Some soldiers ditched the

whole thing, perhaps keeping only a blanket, or not even that.

Toward the end of the war, Confederate and Union veterans alike knew how to pack light, and both found ways to avoid using the knapsack. They rolled up their spare ammo, socks, and undies (if any) in their blanket, tied it up in a big loop, and carried it that way, across one shoulder.

BELOW AND BELOW, LEFT *Confederate soldiers, in particular, learned to do more with less, carrying only the minimum required for sustained operations – a little food, a little water, a lot of ammunition, and not much more.*

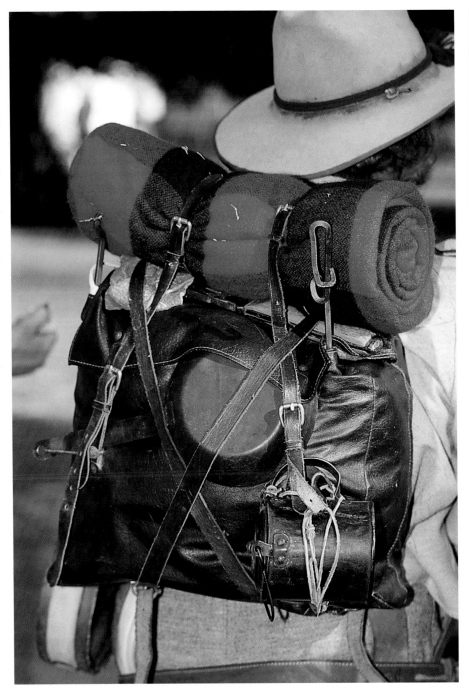

Basic Training

ABOVE, RIGHT *Confederate infantry soldier from the 34th North Carolina Infantry with full kit – musket, haversack, canteen, cartridge box, cap box, and knapsack.*
LEFT *Union "bullseye" canteens were popular items with the soldiers of both sides, as long as they had been well made and the seams didn't leak.*

The process of turning a raw, rank civilian into a proper soldier is a long, stressful, and interesting one, to all parties involved. The same applied during the Civil War, when "camps of instruction" were set up near Richmond, Washington DC, and many other locations in every state, to teach thousands of recruits the basics of soldiering.

Actually, it was more stressful then. There were no standards for training new soldiers, and almost no old soldiers to do the training. There were a few veterans of the Mexican War, but hardly enough to go around. So when war came in April 1861, the flood of aspiring soldiers had to be trained by very novice drill instructors holding copies of *Hardee's Rifle and Light Infantry Tactics*, a little book that served both sides as a guide to the fundamentals.

Typically, Civil War soldiers received their initial training in one of two ways. If they were part of a new regiment, as virtually all were at the outset of the war, they would learn their lessons alongside all the other recruits. The regiment would be ordered en masse to a camp away from the distractions of actual combat, where they received their initial issue of clothing and field equipment, were assigned to a tent or a simple wood-frame barracks, and began the sometimes painful learning process of basic training.

The other, and more painful method of instruction, occurred more commonly later in the war, when new recruits were sent as individuals to old regiments to replace losses suffered in combat or through desertion and disease. Known as "fresh fish," these recruits might go from the recruiting hall to the front line in just a week, if their new regiment was in a combat zone. Their instruction was provided by the veterans, when they had the time and inclination.

Veteran soldiers in combat units have never been very hospitable to replacements, and that was as true in the Civil War as in World War II and later. Raw replacements are dangerous to

themselves and everyone around them, take a lot of extra attention, are unsafe with weapons, and need constant babysitting. Especially during Civil War days, when regiments were recruited from single communities and where everybody in the unit knew each other from the beginning, a replacement from another locale was a real misfit, socially as well as militarily. A certain amount of practical joking at the expense of new men seems always to have been a common aspect of military life, and even today new mechanics fresh from school are sent out for mythical tools, like the elusive "left-handed crescent wrench."

But the advantage of such a system was that the veterans would teach the recruit practical soldiering skills and fieldcraft that he would never learn at a camp of instruction. The old soldiers who had survived passed along all the tricks of the trade, and all the vices, too. But the skills were extremely practical – how to load and fire a musket while lying on the ground, for instance, and the many and varied ways to hide liquor from the officers.

DRILL AND CEREMONY

Basic training during the Civil War was called the "School of the Soldier," the kindergarten of the Army. The process

begins now as it began then, about two seconds after you put up your right hand and swear the oath of enlistment. The new recruit's first lesson is that he doesn't even know how to stand up straight, and the sergeant or officer will soon fix that. Rather suddenly, the recruit starts learning about the fine points of the Position of Attention, then called the Position of the Soldier – heels together, feet at a 45-degree angle and on line, knees straight, head up, shoulders back naturally, eyes directly to the front. The only things different about the position of attention then and now are that the hands were held with the palm slightly to the front, with the little finger along the trouser seam, while today the thumb is against the seam, the palm facing somewhat to the rear. The modern soldier also stares at the horizon, while back then it was at a point on the ground, about 30 feet to the front.

LEFT *A private with his musket at "left shoulder arms" waits for morning roll call.* BELOW, LEFT *Confederate soldiers manning Fort McRee at Pensacola, Florida, form up with their weapons at "shoulder arms."*

HUMORS OF THE CAMP

A soldier at the headquarters of the artillery brigade of the 5th Corps, at Culpepper, Virginia, gives the following account of the amusements at camp:

Almost the only diversion the soldiers have nowadays is derived from the new recruits, constantly arriving. They are the butt of all jokes and the easy prey of all sells and tricks. No class of men enjoy fun more heartily than the soldiers. They squeeze sport out of everything, and seem to have acquired the faculty of ascertaining, intuitively, where most of it is to be found.

On a drill, the new recruit is always sure to get his toes exactly where a "vet" wishes to put the butt of his musket as he "orders arms;" and if there is a mud puddle within a yard of him, he is sure to dress into it.

Capt. Reynolds, of Battery S, 1st New York Artillery, has got a large number of new recruits, and some of the jokes that the Veterans play on them are very amusing. The recruits are constantly sighing over departed luxuries, and are very easily duped into any sell, where the inner man is concerned. A mischievous vet got a whole squad of them out in line the other day, when it was raining quite hard, to receive their ration of "warm bread." One fellow, greener than the rest, was sent to the captain's office for his "ticket for butter." Another went to the company clerk with a two-quart pail for his "three-days' ration of maple sugar."

Recruits have a hard time keeping their eyes to the front, both shoulders equally back, and their feet at the prescribed angle. Instructors are patient men, for the first five or six seconds, but then they tend to yell a lot.

When the recruits start to get the hang of standing up straight in a military manner, they are taught Eyes Right and Eyes Left, and what we call today "parade rest," but for which the command during the Civil War era was simply, "In Place – REST!"

They were brought from the rest position to attention and back again, over and over, until they started to show some precision. Military drill is a carefully choreographed traditional dance, one that takes many rehearsals to learn. It isn't enough simply to know the steps and the moves; they must be done exactly at the same time as all the other men in the squad, platoon, or company.

There are a lot of aspects of drill that, to new recruits and people who haven't served in uniform, seem silly, unnecessary, and unnatural. But even today, and especially during the Civil War, close order drill teaches individual men to work as a team, to pay attention to commands and to respond immediately. Back then, the commands had a practical battlefield application because, particularly at the beginning of the war, soldiers maneuvered and fired by the numbers, on command.

VOICE OF COMMAND

While the novice soldiers were struggling with the fundamentals of military life, their instructors were often learning the fundamentals of command. Keeping control of a gaggle of recruits by voice power alone is such a daunting task that today we send soldiers to an NCO academy to learn how to do it, and it is a challenging task. During the Civil War,

drill instructors learned by experience and observation, and through occasional disasters.

Soldiers quickly learn that almost all commands, including single-word commands, have two parts: the first preparatory, the second for execution. The first part of the command warns you what you're going to do, the second is the order to do it. That's why, when a sergeant brings his men to attention, he mangles the word into something that sounds today like "ATTT-ten – HUT!" Civil War sergeants probably did the same thing, and Civil War soldiers, properly schooled, waited till the very beginning of that last syllable to move. Then, they would promptly bring their heels together, feet at the prescribed 45-degree angle, stand up very straight, and look straight ahead. The sergeant will be listening to the sound of his people executing the order as much as watching it. If the soldiers do it correctly, there is one sharp click as they all come to attention together; if they don't do it together, it sounds and looks ragged and sloppy. Then the sergeant yells at them for a while, walks around and through the ranks, verbally abusing the worst of the lot – perhaps in a rich Irish brogue in many cases back then. After some of this counseling, the Civil War sergeant would command, "In place – REST!" and the soldiers would assume the position of ease for a moment, before trying it again.

The tactical problem of converting recruits into soldiers takes a special soldier or junior officer to do well, just as it did in the Civil War. It requires the ability to control the voice, to project it so every man in the unit can hear, understand, and obey each command, even when they are in the back rank at the end of the file of a full-up company of 100 soldiers.

Naturally, lack of experience and training produced some chaos during these drills; chaos and confusion are old Army traditions. Drill sergeants sometimes got their men into hopeless situations, and one resourceful Confederate NCO solved the problem with the immortal and imaginative command, "Disentangle to the front – MARCH!"

ABOVE, LEFT *Trussed up like a turkey, this Confederate soldier demonstrates "order arms."*
LEFT *Members of the 1st Georgia Infantry, dressed in their best uniforms and white gloves, pose for the camera.*
ABOVE, RIGHT *A Confederate platoon formed up for roll call, weapons at "left shoulder arms."*
RIGHT *The position of "charge bayonet."*

God favors the big regiments, and that's what the Union was able to send to battle — they died by platoons, companies, and battalions, but there were always others to take their place. When properly trained, equipped, and led, soldiers like these put a murderous "weight of metal" downrange.

Foot Soldiers

The vast majority of soldiers on both sides during the Civil War were infantrymen. Their basic mission was to exchange fire with enemy infantry. The problem, particularly in the early phase of the war, was that the tactics of the time didn't account for the awesome firepower of the rifled musket combined with the minie ball. When infantry units presented themselves on line, elbow to elbow, they were often slaughtered. But they learned to use cover and concealment, and to reload lying on their back.

THE REGIMENT

The fundamental Civil War troop organization was the regiment. At the beginning, when they were mustered into service, the regulation infantry regiment was composed of about 1,050 officers and men in ten companies of 104 each. Regular regiments had a complement of between two and four battalions, each of eight companies, or a paper strength of 832 men. The volunteer regiments didn't use the battalion organization and were each required to field ten full companies at their mustering-in.

Each company at full strength, by regulation, comprised 104 people – three officers and 101 enlisted soldiers – organized in two platoons and a small headquarters element. Each platoon was composed of two 20-man sections.

The Standard Federal Company:
• The company commander, a captain;
• Two platoon commanders, a first and second lieutenant;
• A first sergeant, the senior NCO in the company;
• Four sergeants, one for each section;
• Eight corporals, one for each squad of ten men;
• Two musicians, a bugler and a drummer;
• One wagoneer;
• 82 private soldiers.

Of course there was tremendous variation in this basic structure during the evolution of the war, both by regulation and as a result of losses, but this was the ideal for Union companies at the beginning of the war, while Confederate companies were similar.

In addition to the companies, the standard Federal regiment had a command element that, by regulation, was supposed to include:

• The regimental commander, a colonel;
• The assistant regimental commander, a lieutenant-colonel, who generally handled the routine movements of soldiers in the field;
• A major, third in command;
• The regimental sergeant-major, the senior enlisted man and administrator;
• The regimental surgeon-major, responsible for treating the ills of the unit;
• An assistant surgeon;
• One hospital steward, the equivalent of today's medic;
• A commissary sergeant, who ordered and issued all food items for the regiment;
• An adjutant, the top clerk of the regiment and primary disciplinarian;
• A quartermaster officer and quartermaster sergeant, who made all the arrangements for ordering and issuing clothing, weapons, ammunition, and similar supplies;
• Two musicians, a bugler and a drummer.

There was considerable variation in these assignments from one regiment to another, depending on the kind of unit and its parentage, Confederate or Federal. Western Federal regiments, operating with more independence than those in the east,

sometimes had their own ordnance sergeant to maintain their weapons. There were teamsters, ambulance drivers, washerwomen, civilian cooks, a sutler, and occasional prostitutes, too, all potentially part of the regimental family, although not all of them wore Union suits.

Together, the full-up Federal infantry regiment included about 1,014 people, and possibly 1,050 or so. But although there were "slots" for that many soldiers and officers, seldom did a regiment have that number of people in the field, and

RIGHT *Infantry at Fort Lincoln. Wholesale recruitment of black troops began in 1863 after the Emancipation Proclamation, and by the end of the war some 180,000 had joined the Union forces. Joseph Williams from Pennsylvania summed up their commitment: "I must avenge my debasment . . . I will sacrifice everything in order to save the gift of freedom for my race."* BELOW *Veterans of Company C, 112th Ohio Infantry, pose informally sometime during the last months of the war.*

regiments were not maintained at that level on either side. The losses from sickness alone quickly reduced the ranks, and most regiments were lucky to be at 70 percent strength at any time in the field; many were frequently much smaller.

While the regular regiments were maintained by replacement volunteers and draftees (after 1864), the volunteer regiments in Federal service were allowed to decay from combat losses, illness, and desertion until they averaged about half-strength by 1863. Some dwindled to a few dozen men only, fewer than a full-up platoon, and became regiments in name only.

While the Confederacy formed regiments on the same basic model, and considered the regiment to be the fundamental building block of the army, Rebel units didn't bother with battalions and had a simplified five-man

RIGHT *The Regimental Colors and National Standard of the 5th New York Regiment (Zouaves) had seen plenty of action when Lieutenant-General Jubal A. Early attacked Union Major-General Philip H. Sheridan on October 19, 1864, near Middletown, Virginia, in the Shenandoah Valley.*
BELOW *Confederate soldiers prepare to fire a volley. The first rank, having already fired, kneels and reloads.*

headquarters staff – a colonel commanding, his executive officer, a lieutenant colonel, a major, a captain serving as adjutant, and a sergeant-major. They also had slots for a bugler, two medical officers, a commissary officer, a quartermaster, and a chaplain.

Confederate regiments were kept supplied with "fresh fish" throughout the war, as much as possible, by conscription and enlistments, and suffered less from the demoralizing effect of unit shrinkage. Even so, Rebel regiments at the Battle of Chancelorsville in 1863 averaged just 409 officers and men, against Federal regiments that weren't much bigger at 433.

COLOR GUARD

Man for man, the bravest soldiers on the battlefield were the color guard, the regimental color sergeant and eight picked corporals. While the battlefield was a dangerous place for everybody, the color guard's job was very nearly suicidal, and the slaughter of these gallant men on both sides was tragic and widespread.

The regimental colors embodied all the trust and honor of the whole unit. Many flags were manufactured by private companies (e.g., Tiffany & Sons of New York) according to the unit's specifications. It is a myth that women made all these flags. The reverence placed in this flag was nearly religious, and its

loss for any reason was the cause for tremendous shame on the part of all the men of the regiment.

The color sergeant carried the regimental colors on the march and into combat, a position of great honor – and extra pay. Consequently, the man selected for the job was expected to be an exemplary soldier in every way. Normally, he was tall, handsome, and well-groomed. He also had to be of demonstrated bravery and reliability. The color sergeant was considered the "heart and soul" of the regiment.

More than that, he filled the role of today's command sergeant-major, the senior enlisted soldier in a battalion or regiment – the representative of the troops, a conduit to the commander in an age when the separation of the officer ranks and the rank-and-file were much more extreme than today.

The color sergeant reported directly to the assistant regimental commander, a lieutenant-colonel, and worked with him daily, in and out of combat. If there was a problem that was bothering the soldiers – unusually bad food, problems with the mail, and similar gripes – it was the color sergeant who would likely bring them to the commander's attention, not one of the company officers.

If the Civil War soldier was having a serious problem with one of his officers – a platoon leader or company commander

– he could talk to the color sergeant about it, and the problem could find the ear of the regimental commander and possible solution.

In line of battle, the color sergeant carried the colors centered on the battalion line, escorted by the corporals, and near the regimental commander. In the heat and smoke and chaos of the fight, a soldier could look around and maintain his alignment in the assault by reference to the regimental colors held high by the color bearer.

But this visibility, and the role of the regimental flag in the Civil War soldier's sense of honor and propriety, made the color sergeant a bullet magnet. Enemy riflemen might admire his valor at the same time as they concentrated their fire on him. When he fell – and that was almost certain in close contact with the enemy – one of the color corporals would take over, catching the staff before the flag could touch the ground. Quite often, that color bearer would fall, too, and others after him. Sometimes a company or regimental commander would grab the flag and charge forward with it, to almost certain death. Major-General Isaac Stevens died in this manner, carrying the colors of the 79th New York Cameron Highlanders (a regiment he had once commanded, and from whom he had stripped its colors for a while after a

mutiny in 1861) at Chantilly, Virginia, on September 1, 1862. But the slaughter was mostly of sergeants and the brave privates who scooped up the colors and maintained the honor of their units at the price of their own lives.

Just as it was a great honor to carry the regimental colors into battle, it was an even greater honor to capture those of an enemy, and tremendous effort was put into the task. Private Sam Watkins was promoted, much to his surprise, to corporal simply for picking up a Federal color abandoned on the battlefield. And sometimes Federal soldiers were awarded the Medal of Honor, the highest possible decoration then and now, for capturing one from an enemy color bearer in battle, or preventing the loss of their own.

Among the soldiers so decorated was William Carney, a member of the 54th Massachusetts Colored Infantry and the first black soldier to receive the Medal of Honor. At the assault on Fort Wagner, on July 18, 1863, the regimental color sergeant was killed. Carney threw away his weapon, grabbed the flagstaff, and led the assault on the Rebel position, although wounded several times. Another was Private James Adams, of Co. D, 1st West Virginia Cavalry, who captured the colors of the 14th Virginia Cavalry in a fight at Nenevah, Virginia, on November 12, 1863.

BUGLE CALLS

The bugler was the link between the command group and the soldiers, a kind of very-short-range radio that could transmit orders from the "head shed" to the rank-and-file, immediately and across a fairly large area. A division commander could communicate almost instantly with his whole command simply by ordering his bugler to sound the assembly call. The brigade buglers would repeat the signal, and it would be relayed, in turn, by the regimental buglers. In a few minutes, 5,000 or more men would be in formation, under arms and in their brigades, regiments, and companies, ready to move out. You couldn't do it faster with a PRC-77 radio.

Every regiment, no matter how depleted, needed at least two musicians: a drummer and a bugler. The bugle was particularly important for members of a cavalry troop, since often they were dispersed over a much wider area than an infantry company and well beyond the bellowing voice of an old sergeant or lieutenant. The sound of the bugle carries beyond the line of sight and, even in the noise and confusion of battle, can be heard and understood over a distance of at least a quarter mile.

The bugler himself was a somewhat privileged soldier in Federal service. Often quite young, buglers were recruited for their musical ability, then trained before assignment to a regiment and company. Once in the regiment, the bugler reported to the chief trumpeter of the unit. He stayed close to the commander in battle and on the march, but the first sergeant kept him busy in camp with the dozens of routine calls that began at sunrise, or before, and lasted until Tattoo and Taps at about 9:15 pm.

Duties for buglers differed in the infantry, artillery, and cavalry. Each had their own specialized calls adapted to the routine needs of their units, and their equipment varied as well. All the musicians in a cavalry unit, for example, were supposed to be armed with sabers and pistols, but not carbines. Normally, they were exempt from most of the latrine-digging details and similar duties, but were always on call to serve as orderlies to the officers, and they reported

LEFT *The color sergeant carries "Old Glory" into battle.*
RIGHT *Two grimy privates, in light marching order, pose for the camera.*
BELOW *General Ambrose E. Burnside outside a tent draped with the National Flag. (Also prominent are the side-whiskers he gave his name to — "burnsides," now "sideburns.")*

to the chief trumpeter, not the first sergeant of their assigned companies.

All Civil War soldiers, in and out of combat, received their orders all day long from the sound of the bugle. Each soldier had to learn some 40 to 50 different calls, a bewildering assortment for the "fresh fish."

Many were common to all units, Federal and Confederate, but varied a little from an infantry regiment to one of artillery or cavalry. For the infantry, each day began with "Assembly of Buglers" (we hear it played today before a horse race), the Army's alarm clock, at five minutes before 5 am during the summer campaign season, an hour later in winter camp. At the same time, nearby artillery and cavalry units would blow "Reveille." For infantry units, "Reveille" had the same meaning as the "Assembly" call did in the artillery and cavalry – insuring that occasionally everybody was confused.

"Reveille" or "Assembly" ordered the soldiers to fall into ranks, at parade rest, for roll call. As the bugle sounded, the soldiers sang, if their NCOs let them get away with it, some variation on these improvised lyrics:

I can't get 'em up, I can't get 'em up,
I can't get 'em up, I tell you.
I can't get 'em up, I can't get 'em up,
I can't get 'em up at all.

The corporal's worse than the private,
The sergeant's worse than the
corporal,
The lieutenant's worse than the
sergeant,
But the captain's worst of all.

I can't get 'em up, I can't get 'em up,
I can't get 'em up this morning;
I can't get 'em up, I can't get 'em up,
I can't get 'em up today.

As the last notes of the call faded away, the company first sergeant probably growled, "At EASE!" to get them all to shut up and called the roll, duly noting the absences in the ever-present little book that all company NCOs have carried for such purposes since the Peloponnesian Wars.

Immediately after reveille, the soldiers were dismissed momentarily for a few minutes, then the bugler in artillery and cavalry regiments sounded stable call, sending the soldiers to care for their horses. Watering call sent the troopers to the nearest stream with the mounts, then at 7 am breakfast call summoned them to chow.

New recruits quickly learned the sound of drill call, typically at 9 am, summoning the soldiers to the parade

ground for two hours of work with the manual of arms and close-order drill and all the skills of the "School of the Soldier."

In cavalry units, "Boots and Saddles" sent the troopers off to saddle and bridle their mounts, and a half hour later (in camp or during routine training), "To Horse" would find the troopers standing at the heads of their mounts, lined up in ranks for roll call.

When "The General" sounded in camp, Civil War soldiers knew it was time to move, and they arranged themselves in marching order immediately. In a cavalry unit, "Boots and Saddles" would follow, then a few minutes later, "Assembly," and shortly afterwards, "March."

During the day in camp, you'd hear the bugler sound "Assembly of The Guard," "Officers Call," "Assembly of Trumpeters," "Orders for Orderly Sergeants" (at 11 am), and "Dinner Call" for the noontime roll call and meal.

After lunch, the bugler would send the soldiers back to drill at about 1 pm, to the picket line for stable call at 4 pm,

then retreat at 5:30 for another roll call and inspection, followed by the company commander's orders for the following day.

The end of the day in camp concluded with "Tattoo," telling the troops that it was time for bed, and "To Extinguish Lights," the bugle call we know today as "Taps." "To Extinguish Lights," has a beautiful, evocative quality to it, particularly as it echoes over a quiet encampment of men under arms. "Reveille" and "Taps" are still heard on every US Army post every day, although now the bugler is recorded.

Although strictly unofficial, soldiers have invented lyrics for all the bugle calls, and there have been many variations for most of them, some quite bawdy. The soldiers sang these lyrics while the bugler played the call. For example, when the bugler sounded stable call, the cavalry troopers were likely to sing these words as they headed to the picket line:

Come off to the stable, all ye who
are able,
And give your horses some oats
and some corn;

For if you don't do it, your
colonel will know it,
And then you will rue it as sure
as you're born.

The bugle call we know today as "Taps"
is reputed to have several origins. Some
modern historians claim that the melody
and its military use predate the Civil War
by many years, but the most common
version of the story (and the one
promoted by the Army and the Library of
Congress today) is that "Taps" was
developed during the Civil War by
Brigadier General Daniel Butterfield

RIGHT *A Confederate commander and his*
aide-de-camp. Bugle calls were of particular
importance to the cavalry leader in the field
who would use them to command his men.
BELOW *But it was not just the bugle that*
issued commands: drums were also called
upon both in the field and in camp – for
example, in the "Long Roll" that sounded the
"Call to Assembly." Often the two were used
together – as in "Taps."

(commander of the 3rd Brigade, 1st Division, 5th Corps of the Army of the Potomac) and his bugler, Sergeant Oliver Norton, during the Peninsula Campaign of 1862. Butterfield hummed the tune, perhaps based on an earlier melody he had heard, and Norton wrote it down and developed it into a bugle call.

At the time – according to the Army – "Taps" was only used by Butterfield's command as an alternative to the then-current call of "Lights Out," and originally was used simply as the soldier's lullaby in that regiment, followed by a few single drum-beats – the real taps in "Taps."

But the evocative melody was heard far beyond the campground of Butterfield's regiment, and others adopted it as well. Later in the war, it was played at the conclusion of a burial service for a fallen soldier, a use for which it has become traditional (along with the drum beat "Muffled Ruffles"). "Taps" was played by both Union and Confederate buglers, becoming so popular that it was adopted as an official US Army bugle call in 1874.

There are many versions of lyrics to accompany "Taps," but this is the one offered by the US Army today:

Fading light dims the sight,
And a star gems the sky,
gleaming bright.
From afar drawing nigh – falls
the night.

Day is done, gone the sun,
From the lake, from the hills,
from the sky.
All is well, safely rest, God is
nigh.

Then good night, peaceful night,
Till the light of the dawn shineth
bright,
God is near, do not fear – friend,
good night.

BELOW *Drummers and musicians of the 93rd New York Infantry at Balton, Virginia, during 1863. Drummers were often as young as 12, and the last of the survivors died in the 1950s.*

THE INFANTRY COMPANY

The basic maneuver element during the Civil War was the company and its supposed 100 men. If you had been in a Civil War infantry company, the following are some of the kinds of mission your unit would have performed.

On the Picket Line – Guard Duty in Camp

The only way a Civil War unit could maintain security in a combat zone was with a multi-layered ring of sentries alert to danger from without and to anyone attempting to sneak out of the camp. Every established camp and every unit out campaigning posted a strong picket line around the unit to maintain security, and these picket lines could be very strong and deep. Just how strong and deep depended on the terrain and level of threat, but generally the pickets would be in sight of each other.

According to the procedures of the time, three layers of security positions insulated the main force from the enemy: individual sentinels (although commonly referred to as "pickets"), a line of outposts behind the sentinels, and a line of pickets behind the outposts. Behind them was the real defensive line, the grand guards. This critical guard duty could be assigned to a battalion, regiment, or even a division. And sooner or later, each soldier's company was likely to be sent out with its parent unit to provide security for the main body.

The Sentinel Line

At the extreme, out closest to the enemy, was a line of individual sentinels, in sight of each other – about 25 yards apart in good terrain, but closer in heavy cover – and providing mutual support in case of contact with an enemy. Ideally, this extreme defensive line was about two miles from the main body. In the event of attack, the sentinels got off a shot and immediately pulled back to the first rally position, about 200 yards to the rear.

The Outpost Line

This is another ring of security positions, called in the manuals of the time "the line of outposts." These positions were held by between four and six men, half of whom were resting and eating while the others were forward on the sentinel line.

The outpost line was a little refuge for the soldiers on the line of sentinels, a place where they were reasonably safe from the enemy, could build a fire for warmth and cooking, and where they could sleep when off duty.

But at the sound of the first shots from the sentinels, the whole outpost line

would come alive with breathless anticipation – all would wake up, pull on their shoes, and grab their muskets. If the threat was significant, and the sound of shooting and the buzz of minié balls was even moderate, the whole outpost would collapse back on the next line of defense, about 200 yards closer to the main body, the line of pickets.

The Line of Pickets

From the line of pickets, the squads were sent forward to man the outposts and sentinel line. Each picket station supported two squads of soldiers, sending them out in rotation, one on duty while the other rested. This was a more administrative line of positions, well back from the sentinels, and a rally point in case of attack.

Grand Guards

The grand guards, 500 yards behind the line of pickets, were the primary security force for the main body, about a mile from the encamped units and a mile or so from the sentinels. Here was the base of operations for the whole line of pickets and sentinels, and in the event of attack, here was where the whole security force would try to make its stand.

Standing Guard

Standing guard, even in a combat zone when the enemy is in range, is usually mind-numbingly boring. During the Civil War, it was so common for Confederate and Federal units to be in static positions near each other that the pickets developed rather novel relationships. They would fire on each other sometimes and occasionally engage in informal, almost friendly, duels at fairly long range. One soldier would poke his head

ABOVE *Soldiers on both sides often went into battle fully expecting to be killed or maimed. They fought anyway, impelled by a sense of personal honor and bonds of commitment and comradeship with the other men in their unit.*

ORDERS HIS OWN EXECUTION

During the Union siege of Yorktown, Virginia, a newspaper correspondent made the following report:

Last night an officer was shot by one of his own men. The officer, Capt. A. R. Wood, had posted his last picket and left him with this order: "Shoot the first man that approaches from the direction of the rebels, without waiting to ask for the countersign."

It was quite dark, and the officer left the picket and lost his way, wandering from our lines instead of to them. He soon discovered his mistake, and turned back. He approached the soldier to

whom he had given the decisive order.

In the shadow the faithful and quick-sighted private saw the dark figure stealing toward him; in an instant, he raised his piece and shot his own captain through the side. The wound was mortal, and thus it turned out that the officer had given the orders for his own execution.

Picket duty here is most perilous and considering that the safety of the whole army depends on the faithfulness with which this duty is performed, one cannot wonder that those detailed for it are so ready to execute the commands of their superiors.

out from behind a tree and give the enemy picket a momentary target. After the first picket fired, the other had his chance. They might take turns in this way for a while, then give up and call an informal truce, put their muskets away, and amble up to chat with each other.

The truce was local, but could become quite friendly and semi-permanent, until the officer of the guard found out and put a stop to it. Until then, though, Johnny Reb was likely to trade plugs of tobacco for Billy Yank's coffee and sugar. Both Reb and Yank liked to exchange newspapers to see what was being reported by the other side. If the picket lines of opposing forces happened to be on opposite sides of a quiet river or creek, sometimes small sailing vessels were rigged and loaded with trade bait, then pushed into the stream to cross unmanned. Such fraternization was prohibited, but common.

Occasionally these truces became extremely friendly, and there is one report of a young Federal officer crossing the lines and being taken to a dance by Rebel officers, who provided him with civilian clothes and a cover story, before returning him after the party.

CIVILITIES OF WAR

A letter from the Army of the Potomac, dated February 12, 1863, contains the following:

The rebels recently rigged up a plank with a sail and rudder attached, and on top placed a drawer, evidently taken from an old secretary, in which he put two Richmond papers, and on top a half plug of tobacco, with a written request for a *New York Herald*, and stating that "they would come over and have a little chat," if we would pledge our faith. But this sort of intercourse is strictly forbidden on our part.

I returned this morning from a visit to our pickets. Company I, 139th Pennsylvania Volunteers, has a very good location for standing post, but the "Johnny Rebs" are perfectly docile. Night before last, Harry Born, one of our boys, was busily engaged in singing a song entitled "Fairy Bell," and when the time came for the chorus, the four Rebs on the post opposite struck up, drowning Harry's voice almost entirely.

One of the more remarkable examples of this kind of friendly exchange occurred during the campaign around Chattanooga, Tennessee, in November 1863. Captain (later General) Horace Porter told the story:

"One morning, [General Grant] started toward our right, with several staff officers, to make a personal examination of the line. When he came in sight of Chattanooga Creek, which separated our pickets from those

OPPOSITE PAGE, TOP AND BOTTOM *Picket duty was dangerous and dreary, requiring long periods on alert, sometimes in close proximity to the enemy. Opposing pickets could be friendly – swapping news and tobacco – or hostile, swapping bullets.* BELOW *Privates Robert Schindler, Jr. and Charles B. Swinford lie in ambush. These Union soldiers are part of the 3rd Maryland Volunteers. Although heat was a common enemy, the winters could be bitterly cold and present a real health hazard.*

OPPOSITE PAGE, TOP When the opposing force decided to move, the picket sounded the alert with his musket – carefully aimed or a hasty shot. A single shot didn't receive much attention – but the spattering sound of many shots, particularly in a rising tempo, would turn out the main body without the formality of a bugle call.

OPPOSITE PAGE, BELOW Scouts and guides of the Army of the Potomac – civilians who helped the army find its way in an era before reliable maps.

BELOW Heavy cover in Virginia and the Carolinas often made it difficult for pickets to see very far, and easy for enemy patrols to approach close enough to bag a few prisoners.

of the enemy, he directed those who accompanied him to halt and stay out of sight while he advanced alone, which he supposed he could do without attracting much attention. The pickets were within hailing distance of each other and had established a temporary truce on their own responsibility, and the men of each army were allowed to get water from the same stream without being fired upon by those on the other side. A sentinel of our picket-guard recognized General Grant as he approached and gave the customary cry, 'Turn out the guard – commanding general!' The enemy on the other side of the creek evidently heard the words, and one of his sentinels cried, 'Turn out the guard – General Grant!' The confederate guard took up the joke, and promptly formed, facing our line, and presented arms. The general returned the salute by lifting his hat, the guard was then dismissed, and he continued on his ride toward our left. We knew

that we were engaged in a civil war, but such civility largely exceeded our expectations."

But most picket duty was uneventful – four hours on post, four hours off, around the clock. At night, in the rain, with the enemy prowling around, it could be exhausting. Even on pleasant days and nights, there was always the prospect of an enemy sniper or squad sneaking up and making a local attack, and it was common for pickets to be killed or captured in this way.

Driving in the Pickets

Sooner or later, though, the enemy attacked, and the first phase of battle was inevitably described as the process of driving in the pickets. When the attack happened, the sentinels would be the first to feel the pressure. They would see the enemy's cavalry or lead elements of infantry on the move toward their own position, perhaps at long range, in open terrain, or just a few hundred yards away.

Immediately, the sentinels with eyes on the enemy would open fire. Their single shots would not do a thing to stem the tide, but they would alert all the other sentinels along the line, who would wake

up and start paying closer attention. If they had the enemy in sight, too, they would also open fire, and perhaps be fired upon. Without bothering much to reload, the sentinels would rally on the line of outposts about 50 yards to the rear.

Those first spattering shots would get the attention of the whole security force, which would go on the Civil War version of Red Alert. If the attack was at all serious, the outpost-line personnel would get their shots in, then rally back to the line of pickets. When the corporal in charge of each of these little positions had a reliable report of contact with the enemy, he would send a runner or mounted courier back to the officer of the guard with a report.

By this time, the tempo of fire was likely to have picked up. The sound of the gunfire would be a clue to the whole security force and main body that something was up. If they heard a few isolated shots, then quiet, they would go back to sleep. But they all listened carefully when it began because if the volume of fire and its tempo increased, everybody knew that either a fight or a flight would happen soon.

The picket line would try to slow the attackers and force them into line of battle, if they could, but it took a lot of firepower to do that. They would fall back to the parent unit, the line of grand guards, and the whole security force would quickly deploy in line of battle, ready to meet the assault.

While the grand guards tried to delay the enemy attack, the main body would be breaking camp, tossing its knapsacks in a pile, and listening to the drummer sound the "Call for Assembly," the "long roll." The whole security element – battalion, regiment, or division – may have been sacrificed to the enemy, buying time, but the main body should have had about an hour to get itself together and into line of battle.

Advanced Guard

When a Civil War force went on the campaign trail, normally it did so in at least division strength, and typically as a corps of two or three divisions. Way out in front of this marching mass of combat power would be the advanced guard of two or three soldiers. A short distance behind them was the rest of their platoon, and behind them a company or battalion, guarding the leading edge of the formation from threats on the line of march.

The soldiers on advanced guard had to be alert to the enemy, who might be waiting to spring an ambush from every ravine and wood line. If they had some cavalry with them, the job was faster and easier – the troopers could scout ahead and off to the flanks much more efficiently than the foot soldiers.

Ideally, in open country, the whole column could move along at a mile-and-a-half or two miles per hour, average. That's a slow stroll in the country if it is sustained, but the pace was slow because of frequent halts while the advanced guard checked out potential threats.

Normally behind the lead element was a senior staff officer or perhaps the commander himself, keeping the advance moving – and staying out of the clouds of dust that enveloped the men farther back in the column. If the commander was back in the column, mounted couriers accompanied the point element to carry back situation reports.

Flankers

An enemy force, large or small, will often attempt to sneak in and attack a moving column from the flanks. Even a tiny band of well-positioned soldiers can create

havoc in a larger force if they spring their ambush skillfully, and if they attack from a well-selected and prepared position, sometimes they can defeat a much larger force.

So flankers protect the main body of the column by patrolling the countryside parallel to the line of march, a kind of extended skirmish line ready to fend off a sudden appearance of enemy cavalry or guerillas. They are a form of moving guard, ready to warn of a threat and delay, not defeat, an assault.

Today, this mission is performed primarily with helicopters and light armored vehicles, but during the Civil War it was a chore for the foot soldiers and for the cavalry. Whole companies, battalions, and regiments were assigned to provide flank security on the move, and it was an exhausting business. While the main body marched down the dusty or muddy road, the flankers were off to the right and left, stumbling through the bushes, climbing over fences, and in and out of ravines.

Rear Guard

Finally, nothing ruined a good retreat after a battle better than a determined

attack by cavalry from the rear. The marching column would have a company, regiment, or more, at the dusty end of the main body, keeping an eye on the road astern. In the event a cavalry force overtook them, they would deploy across the line of march and attempt to turn back, or at least delay, the attack.

If the attack was determined, the rear guard would be gobbled up and a rout develop. Then, the pursuers simply rode up the column, taking prisoners, cutting men down with their sabers, and shooting them until they became tired or ran out of ammunition. This happened many times during the Civil War.

ONE SOLDIER'S STORY

In many ways, Private Luke Hope, of Company C, 110th Ohio Volunteer Infantry, was typical of the Civil War Union soldier, and of the Confederate soldier, too. With wife Mary, sons Christopher and James, and his extended family, he emigrated from Ireland prior to the war. They all settled in Ohio, in what was then the west. At 44, Luke was too old to be prime soldier material during the early years of the war, but by late 1863, the bounty for enlistment was a tempting

ABOVE, LEFT *Union pickets advance warily before the main forces assemble. Note the carbine carried by the soldier in contrast to the rifles carried by the bulk of the forces.*
ABOVE *The last thing a soldier might see was the muzzle flash of the musket that killed him.*
RIGHT *Two corporals and a private ready to hit the trail. Their muskets have "sword" bayonets fixed – useful implements for almost anything except attacking the enemy.*

$300, so he and his two sons (then 18 and 21) enlisted in Company C (Capt. H. H. Stevens, commanding), 110th Ohio Volunteer Infantry. That was on January 21, 1864, at the recruiting office in Columbus. Luke's enlistment papers read:

"I, Luke Hope, born in Ireland, aged forty-four years and by occupation a laborer, do Hearby Acknowledge to have volunteered this Twenty-Fifth day of January, 1864 to serve as a Soldier in the

ARMY OF THE UNITED STATES OF AMERICA, for the period of three years unless sooner discharged by proper authority; Do also agree to accept such bounty, pay, rations, and clothing, as are, or may be, established by law for volunteers. And I, Luke Hope do solemnly swear, that I will bear true faith and allegiance to the United States of America, and that I will serve them honestly and faithfully against all their enemies or opposers whomsoever; and that I will observe and obey the orders of the President of the United States, and the officers appointed over me, according to the Rules and Articles of War."

He was, like quite a few of his new comrades, barely able to sign his name and might not have been able to read. The enlistment papers were endorsed by Captain James Wilcox, the recruiting officer, and Sergeant C. H. Osborne. At the bottom of the form, Osborne endorsed the statement that reads:

"I Certify on Honor, that I have minutely inspected the Volunteer, Luke Hope, previously to his enlistment, and that he was entirely sober when enlisted: that, to the best of my judgment and belief, he is of lawful age: and that, in accepting him as duly qualified to perform the duties of an able-bodied soldier, I have strictly observed the Regulations which govern the recruiting service. This soldier has Brown eyes, Dark hair, Fair complexion, is Five feet Eight inches high."

They paid him $60 of his $300 bounty, plus $13 advance on his regular pay.

Luke's initial clothing issue included one jacket, one pair of trousers, a greatcoat, fatigue cap, two flannel

undershirts, two flannel drawers, two pairs of really bad wool socks, and a blanket, haversack, knapsack, and canteen. Once he arrived at Company C, he was issued his weapons and accoutrements – musket, cartridge belt, cap box, cartridge box, and bayonet.

That $73 was the last pay he would get to enjoy, because Luke soon became chronically ill. By February, he had started suffering from a series of attacks of chronic diarrhea that sent him to the hospital, usually at De Camp General Hospital, on David's Island in New York Harbor, for periods during June, July, August, and September, although he wasn't so sick that he wasn't occasionally

MAIN PICTURE *Confederate infantry fire at the approaching Union Army at the Battle of Sailor's Creek, just 30 miles east of the quiet town of Appomattox, Virginia. The battle took place on April 6, 1865, only three days before General Robert E. Lee surrendered to General Ulysses S. Grant at Appomattox Court House.*
INSET *In line of battle, the first rank primes its weapons with much less precision than on the parade ground.*

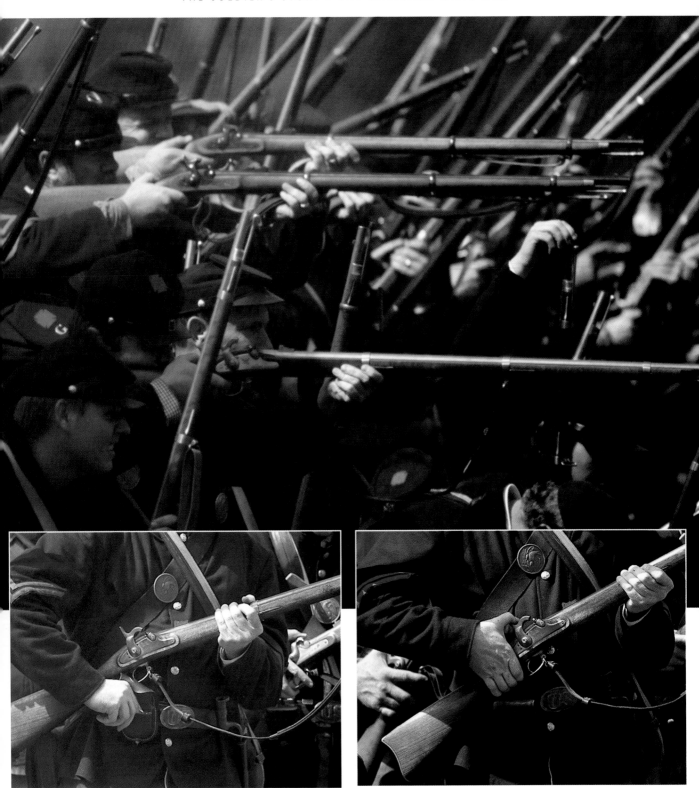

available for service. He was wounded in battle at Cedar Creek, Virginia, when the 110th was heavily involved in combat, but was off to the military hospital again in November and December.

The Army tried to discharge him in mid-January, but he was too sick to move. He died exactly one year to the date of his enlistment and was buried there by the hospital. His son, also named Luke, signed for his belongings – the same ones he'd been issued a year before: a greatcoat, haversack, a pair of shoes, one shirt, a pair of trousers, a vest, cap, and $30 in cash.

Of the two sons who enlisted with him, James was captured on June 15, at Winchester, Virginia, sent to Libby Prison, and later exchanged in time to get back to the 110th and be wounded at Cedar Creek: he survived to be mustered out with the rest of Company C on 25 June. Christopher took a bullet in the hand and side, from which he recovered, and was captured during the Battle of the Wilderness, May 6, 1864. He was paroled a month later, and mustered out in June 1865. None of the Hopes, apparently, ever got the rest of their $300 enlistment bounty.

WEAPONS

The outset of the war found the North, particularly, poorly armed and equipped, and – after the capture of the machinery at the Harper's Ferry arsenal – desperate for weapons. The militias and state guard units already had weapons, but they were generally old and obsolete.

Muskets and Rifles

The Civil War came at an interesting point in the development of the long infantry weapon, in the transition period between the old-fashioned musket – an unrifled,

muzzle-loaded smoothbore – and the rifled breech-loader. Some muskets were rifled, making them rifle- (or rifled-) muskets such as the Springfield (see below).

If you had been one of the patriots of 1860 or '61, you might have been issued a Model 1816 musket, an ancient relic of a design very similar to the weapons used during the Revolutionary War eight decades before. Almost one million of these guns had been made and were available for issue by state armories and militias. Some still retained the old flintlock ignition system, although many had been converted to percussion by the onset of the war.

Even worse were the cheap imports, heavy, crude smoothbores from Europe. These things were brutal when they fired – to the shooter, not the shootee, who was notoriously safe from the large projectiles. Even so, a lot of Johnny Rebs and Billy Yanks marched off to battle with these old smoke-poles at right-shoulder-shift.

If you had been a little more fortunate, or waited a few months to enlist, you might have been given a Model 1842 smoothbore musket, or perhaps the rifled conversion of the same weapon. A quarter million of these had been made between 1842 and '55 and, along with the M1816/1822 musket, they were all that was available in quantity till about 1863.

These were rather loathsome weapons – almost five feet long, with a huge .69cal bore. The Model 1822 and 1842 muskets, like most other long guns of the period, weighed about nine pounds. They kicked like a mule and were notoriously inaccurate. The design omitted a rear sight, so you simply pointed the thing in the general direction of the target, rather like a big shotgun, closed your eyes tight, and jerked the trigger.

These smoothbore muskets were used like shotguns, too. They couldn't reliably hit a man-sized target at more than 50 yards or so, and their unpatched projectiles allowed a lot of the propellant gasses to escape, reducing muzzle velocity and, consequently, range and stopping power.

The standard load for the smoothbores was a ball or "buck-and-ball" (one ball the

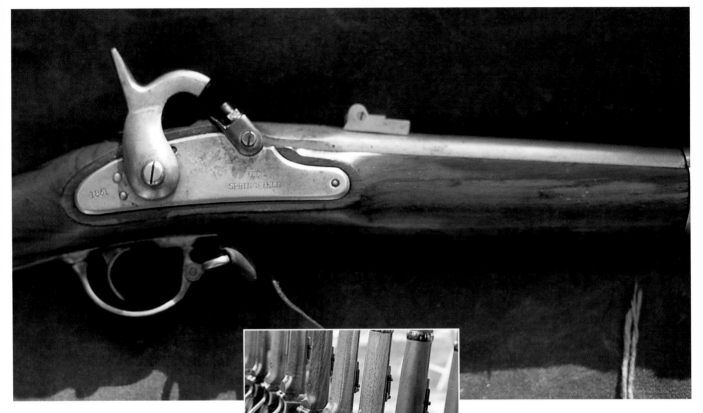

size of the bore, plus three smaller buckshot about one quarter-inch in diameter). They were "area" weapons, useful only against massed troops at short range (under 200 yards) or against individual enemy soldiers at VERY short range (under 50 yards). Beyond 200 yards, the round ball's trajectory and retained energy dropped to almost nothing.

For both sides, these old weapons had two prime virtues during the first years of the war: they were available, and they threw a massive chunk of lead downrange. If you shot somebody with a lead ball nearly three-quarters of an inch in diameter at close range, it was a bit like hitting him with a small cannonball – and he tended to stay shot.

Model 1861 Rifle-Musket
But then came the classic weapon of the Civil War, the Model 1861 rifle-musket. Often known as the Springfield musket because of its initial production at the Springfield, Massachusetts, armory, this simple, sturdy weapon was the state of the art for military long guns of the time.

Although it closely resembled the earlier smoothbore muskets, this new long arm represented a radical change in weapon technology, and that, in turn, produced radical changes in tactics and the effectiveness of infantry. A rifled bore combined with a new kind of projectile made the weapon far more accurate, with longer range and higher velocity. That meant that a trained, skilled infantry soldier could reliably hit a man-sized target with his first shot at 100 yards if he

TOP *The M1861, and its many variants, was the last, best example of the muzzle-loading military weapon – sturdy, powerful, accurate, reliable, effective, and almost, but not quite, "soldier-proof."*
ABOVE *Sharps carbines. The Sharps was a well-tested and effective weapon, the first popular American military breechloader, and commonly used by cavalrymen.*
RIGHT *Rifle-muskets ready for action.*

was given time to aim – a "probability of kill," or "PK" as we call it today, of nearly 100 percent under good conditions.

That accuracy and hitting power extended out to 400 yards, although you couldn't expect to drop your man with the first shot. But now the infantry soldier had a folding rear sight, with notches for ranges up to 400 yards, that allowed him to seriously engage enemy soldiers, as individuals and groups, at long range.

Spencer Rifle
The Spencer helped modernize warfare upon its introduction in 1863. Instead of requiring the bullet and powder to be loaded through the muzzle, the .52cal. Spencer used fully self-contained metallic cartridges in a tubular magazine housed in the butt of the weapon. Seven cartridges, plus one in the chamber, made a single rifleman a potent source of firepower on the battlefield, and the rifleman could carry half a dozen preloaded tubular magazines in a case, ready to go, much like the detachable magazines used on modern military rifles. Although long and clumsy for cavalry work, the Spencer in its initial rifle format nonetheless got a workout with the cavalry until a shorter carbine model was produced.

A skilled rifleman could put 21 aimed rounds downrange per minute, if he had the preloaded tubular magazines, and this firepower, along with the weapon's other virtues, made a tremendous impression on both sides of the war, helping to change battle tactics. Twelve thousand of the rifle version were produced for Union infantry forces, plus another 94,000 carbines for the cavalry.

Henry Lever-Action Rifle
Also used by infantry and a few cavalry units later in the war was the excellent lever-action Henry. This .44cal weapon, the forerunner of the legendary Winchester repeating rifle, carried 16 cartridges in a tubular magazine under the barrel. The US government purchased only 1,731 Henrys, but many soldiers bought them with their own money at

about $40 each, a very substantial sum for a private soldier. It was long and heavy for an infantry weapon, but all that firepower made it attractive.

The Amazing Minié Ball

The radical improvement in the effectiveness of the new rifles was the direct result of an improved kind of bullet, known as the minié ball. This elongated projectile, similar to the classic bullet shape we know today, had a kind of skirt around its hollow base.

Rifles had been around for a long time before the minié ball, and their accuracy could be phenomenal. But early rifles were slow to load because their round bullets had to be patched with a small piece of cloth, which engaged the rifled bore and imparted spin to the projectile when it was fired.

The minié ball did away with the patch. Black powder (typically about 70 grains of FFG grade) was poured down the bore, then the minié ball popped in the muzzle and rammed home. When the rifle was fired, the propellant gasses expanded the soft lead skirt of the bullet, sealing the bore against leakage and engaging the rifling. The bullet spun down the tube and off downrange on its grand adventure, with precision and velocity. Its massive weight absorbed a lot of energy, giving it a killing impact at ranges of a mile and more.

In early tests with the minié ball, a soldier was directed to load and fire as fast as he reasonably could. He got off ten shots in five minutes, and put six of them on target (a two-and-a-half-foot square) at 100 yards. Then, taking his time, he put ten out of ten in a target just one-foot square at the same range, and the same into a two-and-a-half-foot square target, 300 yards out. He achieved one hit on a four-foot square target at 500 yards.

HOW TO SHOOT THE MODEL 1861 SPRINGFIELD RIFLE-MUSKET

In the Army, there are two ways to do anything – the Army way and your sergeant's way. You learn both at the first opportunity, and carefully avoid confusing them.

The Army way of shooting the M1861 rifle or any of its muzzle-loading variants was, of course, "by the numbers." Soldiers learned this drill almost as soon as they enlisted and drew their basic issue. For all of the war, and for both sides of the conflict, the ritual was based on a book called *Hardee's Tactics*. And it made sense for teaching raw recruits how to handle a weapon without causing too many innocent casualties.

Actually, the recruits to the "blue" and "gray" were often extremely inept with weapons of any kind, and a large

number of them died from training accidents with weapons. Recruits learned the musket firing drill by the numbers from endless repetition before being given a chance to load and fire ball ammunition. Here's what you would have needed to know to keep the sergeant happy:

At the command, "LOAD!" and from the position of shoulder arms, bring the rifle from the shoulder smoothly to the ground, just in front of your body, at the same time extending the right foot slightly, the heel against the arch of the left foot. The butt of the rifle is captured by the "V" formed by your feet, keeping it under control. The weapon's barrel is away from you, the ramrod nearest your face. Hold the rifle with your left hand at the middle barrel band. While still facing forward and still at a modified position of attention, reach over to the cartridge box on your right hip, lift the flap, and open it – and wait for the command:

"Handle – CARTRIDGE!" On the command of execution, grasp a cartridge in the box (you will have to find it by touch),

grasp it with the thumb and next two fingers only, and raise the cartridge to your mouth with the paper tail between your teeth. Your sergeant will command:

"Tear – CARTRIDGE!" Bite off the end of the cartridge, being careful to hold the thing vertical and avoid spilling much of the powder. Inevitably, you will get some in your mouth, the dubious flavours of sulphur, charcoal, and potassium nitrate adding a little spice to the experience. Move the open cartridge to the front of the muzzle, palm turned inward, ready to pour the powder down the tube. Wait for the command:

"Charge – CARTRIDGE!" With your elbow at shoulder level and eyes fixed firmly on the muzzle, rotate the hand to pour the powder smartly into the tube. Shake the cartridge, then push it into the muzzle, bullet right side up, and keep your hand in that position till you get the next command. If you spill much – and you will at first – Old Sarge will yell at you. He will yell at you anyway, so wait for the next command:

"Draw – RAMMER!" This is a three-step maneuver. First, grasp the end of the rammer with just your thumb and forefinger. Don't use the other fingers, or you will hear about it. Smartly extract the rammer part way, reverse the right hand, and pull it all the way out. Properly done, the rammers of the men in the second rank just graze the shoulders of the men in the first, and you end up with the ramrod poised above the muzzle, ready for the next command:

"Ram – CARTRIDGE!" With thumb and forefinger of your right hand only, grasp the ramrod at its end and smartly ram the bullet and the remains of the paper down the bore. Ram twice, insuring that the bullet is seated firmly on top of the powder, not halfway down the barrel.

At the command, "Return – RAMMER!" you pull the ramrod out, grab it in the middle with thumb and forefinger, palm downward, and extract it completely from the bore. Then, rotate the rammer 180 degrees, position the end of the rod just above the first pipe, with your eyes firmly fixed on the pipe. Insert the rod, push it down and

ABOVE, RIGHT, AND OPPOSITE PAGE *Loading the rifle-musket begins by withdrawing a cartridge from the box, tearing the paper with the teeth, and pouring the charge down the bore. Then the projectile and the remnants of the paper cartridge are stuffed into the bore, the ramrod withdrawn and reversed, and the bullet rammed until it is seated at the bottom of the bore.*

ABOVE *At the command "Fire!" the first rank cuts loose at the enemy. The massed fire of a platoon or company, directed at a specific target like a gun crew or platoon, could be extremely effective – if smoke didn't obscure their aim and the riflemen didn't panic.*

LEFT *Privates Tim Moore and Robert Young, 54th Massachusetts Volunteer Infantry, Company B – of Glory fame – represent the men that defended their nation.*

ABOVE, RIGHT *This photograph is staged, but the ambulance and its litter-bearers are real enough. Casualty evacuation and battlefield medicine were new concepts at the beginning of the war, and highly polished skills at the end.*

seat it fully with the thumb. Then shift hand positions so that your left hand drops to the forestock, just in front of the trigger guard, the right still at the muzzle, holding the end of the rammer. Now the sergeant commands:

"PRIME!" This is a two-step command. First, raise the rifle with your left hand, grasping the weapon at its natural balance point, at the same time dropping your right hand to the grip, forefinger on the lock plate, and bring your right foot back to form a 45-degree angle with the left. Then, pivot to the right on the left foot and bring the weapon down simultaneously so that it is held naturally in front of the body, muzzle raised and to the left, right hand on the grip (the position called "Charge – BAYONET").

Then, use the thumb of your right hand to bring the hammer back to the half-cock position. Support the rifle with the left hand while extracting a cap from the cap box on the belt's right side. Place the cap firmly on the nipple cone and press it on with the thumb. At this stage, the weapon is almost ready to fire.

At the command, "READY!" draw the hammer all the way back to full cock.

At the command, "AIM!" bring the butt of the rifle to the small of the shoulder, right index finger on the trigger, right elbow elevated, and align the sights on the target.

At the command, "FIRE!" squeeze the trigger – don't jerk it! – and the weapon discharges, sending its little missive downrange. Continue to hold the rifle in this position till you hear the next command, which is likely to be "Shoulder – ARMS!"

Well, that's the way it was supposed to be done, and that's the way you would have learned to do it by daily drill in camp. But in actual combat, this drill (like so many others) deteriorated badly. The first few volleys of a skirmish or a battle might have been executed by command, but soon enough the order would have been, "FIRE AT WILL!" and each man would have been loading and firing as fast and effectively as he could.

Sometimes that wasn't very effective at all. Infantry soldiers were notoriously bad shots. The officers and NCOs constantly reminded the men, "Aim low!" because it was common for rifle fire to pass over the heads of the opposing team.

Troops in their first battles are known for their dangerous anxiety. During the muzzle-loading era, occasionally that resulted in a soldier loading one round on top of another, forgetting after each to place a cap on the nipple. Ancient and rusty muskets have been dug up on battlefields stuffed to the gills with one minié ball on top of another.

Another result of undisciplined fire occurred when a soldier forgot to put the ramrod back in its housing under the barrel. That's when the metal rod went flying across the battlefield – and all observers, on both sides, said to themselves, "Somebody out there is an idiot!"

Today, a single rifle shot will have battalions of soldiers taking cover. The Civil War soldier was expected to stand up, no matter how bad the fire, unless ordered to do otherwise. There was a reason for this that isn't immediately obvious: the Springfield and all other muzzle-loaders were very difficult to load except from a standing position. The weapons could be loaded from a prone position, but the process was slow and awkward.

GOOD SHOOTING

The color bearer of the 10th Tennessee (Irish) having been shot down in the battle of Chickamauga, the colonel ordered one of the privates to take the colors. Pat, who was loading at the time, replied, "By the holy St. Patrick, Colonel, there's so much good shooting here, I haven't a minute's time to waste fooling with that thing!"

THE EFFECTIVENESS OF RIFLE FIRE IN BATTLE

As good as the Springfield rifle was during testing, there was another, more practical, test to come for weapon and soldier. Combat is a very strange experience. Its effects vary from one individual to another. The biggest, toughest soldier beforehand may be reduced to a quivering wreck before anybody fires a shot near him. The little wimpy guy can turn out to be the hero of the day, a steady stalwart under fire and occasionally capable of great valor. Frequently, both types, and all between, were awful shots during the Civil War.

There's an old military adage that says it takes a man's weight in lead to kill him, and statistically, that's the way it worked out when Yank and Reb exchanged fire. Thanks to detailed records, William Fox was able to report that during the Battle of Stone's River (December 29, 1862, to January 2, 1863) the Federal infantry fired two million rounds of musket ammunition (artillery wounds were calculated separately) that killed and wounded 13,832 Confederate soldiers. That equates to 145 rounds of rifle fire alone for each hit – not quite a man's weight, but still an awful lot of lead.

ABOVE *Lead ranks of the Army of the Potomac approach the site of the Battle of Cedar Creek near Belle Grove Plantation. The battle took place on October 19, 1864, when Confederate General Early's Army of the Shenandoah Valley attacked the Federal forces commanded by Union General Sheridan.*

RIGHT *An engraving of the assault on Petersburg captures some of the intensity of the moment in the days before combat photographers went into battle with the troops.*

M60 machine-gun, and like the machine-gun, that infantry company tended to be used as what we call today an "area" weapon, delivering suppressive fire. They fired at an enemy company, for example, drawn up in line of battle perhaps 200 yards or more distant, or at an enemy artillery gun crew 500 yards or more across the field. While the odds of one man hitting one of the horses or gun crew were pretty slim, they were 100 times better when the whole company fired at the same target, and that's how they were often used.

The Civil War rifleman couldn't see his target clearly because the battlefield he fought on was a perfect illustration of the concept of the "fog of war." There was so much smoke and dust that it was impossible to see anything more than a few yards away with much clarity. That was one reason musket fire was so ineffective. Much of it was based on the "spray and pray" principle; often a waste of ammunition.

THE BAYONET

If you asked a Civil War soldier how to use the bayonet in combat, his answer is likely to have been, "Don't." It just wasn't (and isn't) a good idea, and Civil War soldiers on both sides knew this very well. When the war was over and the statistics for all the kinds of wound were tallied, it was revealed that almost nobody (in a statistical sense) was hurt with those bright, intimidating bayonets you see in all the photographs. Here's why.

First, you have to get VERY close to make it work at all, and that makes it easy for the other guy to shoot or stick you, too. Second, you have to confront the guy in a very intimate way, something that is morally more difficult than popping him with a rifle at 50 yards. Besides that, the whole thing tends to be sloppy, noisy, smelly, and generally distasteful. And, the damn blade can easily get stuck in bone or cartilage, and you have to put your foot on the squirming, squealing guy while you try to pull the thing back out. It doesn't kill quickly, or cleanly, or sometimes at all. Worse still, you get to remember the look on the guy's face when you're done.

However, the bayonet is great to hold a candle in your tent at night, or to turn your musket into a tent pole, or a digging

ABOVE *Three soldiers and their well-worn sergeant (complete with notebook, just like today) pose for the camera.*
LEFT *There were seldom enough of them, but ambulance attendants were assigned the difficult job of casualty evacuation. Hat and arm bands identified them and their role, and helped prevent charges of desertion when these men were found behind the lines.*
RIGHT *Federal forces fire on Confederate lines at Sailor's Creek, just prior to General Lee's surrender at Appomattox Court House a few days later.*

However, when a man or a company settled down, learned to ignore the buzzing of enemy fire going by and the patter of lead hail falling nearby, the Springfield rifle could be murderously effective.

One man was expected to fire two rounds per minute, average, in battle. Thus a full-up infantry company of 100 men would deliver a respectable weight of fire of 200 rounds per minute. That's the same weight of sustained fire as today's

implement, or something with which to roast your "liberated" bacon. Soldiers on both sides avoided using it in combat because they all knew the same thing – bayonets are dangerous.

SHARPSHOOTERS

While most soldiers on both sides of the issue used their rifles as "area" weapons, a few were expert shots, able to pick off high-priority targets like officers, artillery crews, color bearers, and pickets at long range and with good first-round kill probability. On the Union side, these were members of Hiram Berdan's two regiments of sharpshooters and other specialized organizations. The Confederates had similar units of their own.

Berdan had been a national champion marksman for many years before the war, a time when precision shooting was a very popular sport in America. At the outset of the war, he was authorized to organize a regiment of carefully selected riflemen for scouting and flank protection missions. Berdan held try-outs for the unit, visiting infantry and other regiments of the regular army and militia, and he had lots

of applicants. The test involved two sequences of fire, both at a target within a ten-inch circle. A prospective soldier fired ten rounds at the target from a rest, at a range of 200 yards, then another ten at an identical target from the standing, off-hand position, at 100 yards. All ten shots in each string had to be within the circle – a very high standard even today with modern military weapons using iron sights.

Apparently, many of the successful applicants had been competitive shooters before the war and used their privately owned match rifles for the test – precision weapons utterly unsuited to military use, except in the most extreme situations.

Berdan got his thousand marksmen, and yet another. But all were difficult to manage and the despair of their brigade commander, who once said of them, "The 2nd U. S. Sharpshooters is the best marching and best fighting regiment I ever saw, but they are so saucy that no one can do anything with them." They had tremendous confidence in their capabilities, an independent attitude, and sometimes contempt for the regulars.

This "saucy" attitude became apparent early. At first, the Union command attempted to issue the 1st and 2nd US Sharpshooters the standard Springfield rifle-musket. They would have none of it, demanding repeating rifles. Initially, these took the form of Colt revolving rifles, a variant of the highly successful pistol design. In rifle form, however, the concept wasn't so successful. Berdan's 1st and 2nd Sharpshooters were issued the weapon, but found it to be complicated and dangerous. If you didn't seal the front of each chamber with grease after reloading, the blow-by gasses from a shot could fire one or more of the other chambers in the cylinder, spitting out up to six bullets all at once. If that happened with a pistol (and it did), the shooter received a tremendous jolt, but no injury; with his left hand in front of the cylinder on the rifle, however, he was in real danger of blowing off his hand.

The regiments of sharpshooters demanded the .52cal Sharps breechloader instead and, in their traditional saucy way, nearly mutinied. This had the

desired effect and they received the Sharps.

The Sharps had been around since 1848 and was a superb weapon, capable of a high rate of fire, but it was complicated. The latter consideration prevented it from superseding the muzzle-loading Springfield and its ilk, but it was well enough known that some soldiers took their own to war. One of these was a famous marksman, Private Truman Head, known as "California Joe." Head bought a New Model 1859 Sharps in 1861, a basic version of the Sharps with a single trigger and saber-type bayonet.

Unlike the Springfield, the Sharps loads from the breech. The trigger guard acts as a lever that drops a massive breech block, exposing the breech of the weapon. A prepared round – a large lead bullet with a linen or paper cartridge backed with 80 grains of coarse black powder – is stuffed in the chamber, then the trigger guard rotated back into position. This raises the breech block, sealing the chamber and nipping a bit off the back of the cartridge at the same time. The shooter puts a musket cap on the cone, pulls the hammer back to full cock, and is ready to fire.

This system has many advantages over the Springfield and similar weapons. For starters, you can load much faster – ten shots per minute sustained fire with the Sharps, as opposed to just two or three with the Springfield. And you don't need to load from an exposed, standing position, as required by a muzzle-loader, allowing you to fight from good cover and concealment. The Sharps rifles were quite accurate, high-velocity, long-range weapons, too – just the ticket for picking off enemy commanders at ranges of 300 or 400 yards.

ABOVE, RIGHT *Berdan Sharpshooters were well-disciplined marksmen, but were used primarily as expert skirmishers. Their Sharps rifles permitted a much larger volume of fire than the standard rifle-musket, helping to make the Berdans highly effective on the battlefield.*
RIGHT *The Berdans were issued a special green uniform and this elegant knapsack and mess kit, supplied by Tiffany's.*
LEFT *Berdan sharpshooters were much more numerous and flexible than the Confederate Whitworth sharpshooters, and operated as highly skilled light infantry, appearing unexpectedly and pouring a high volume of well-aimed and effective fire into enemy units.*

FATAL LAST WORDS

The history of warfare is filled with famous quotations, including the immortal words of Union Major General John Sedgwick. On May 19, 1864, during the battle at Spotsylvania, Sedgwick found some of his artillerymen pinned down by sniper fire from the Rebel lines, about 800 yards away. With his aides, he rode up to the gun crews, who were cowering behind any cover they could find as the bullets whizzed and whined through the air, and exhorted them with the quote for which he will forever be remembered:

"What! What! Men dodging this way for single bullets! I am ashamed of you. They couldn't hit an elephant at this distance …"

The bullet hit Sedgwick just below the left eye and he fell from his horse, not quite, but soon to be, dead. The shot has been attributed to Private Charlie Grace and to Private Ben Powell, both of whom apparently fired on Sedgwick and his staff officers at about the same time. This single shot had a tremendous psychological effect on the Federal soldiers – just as the Rebel snipers intended.

Berdan's saucy soldiers demanded the Sharps, and Berdan got it for them. Their rifles were equipped with dual "set" triggers normally used on target weapons, adjustable so that a very light pressure would release the hammer.

The US Sharpshooters received special treatment in everything else, too. Their uniforms were a distinctive dark green with black buttons, both designed to help the soldier blend into the woodwork. Their knapsacks came from Tiffany in New York – calfskin with the hair on – at a cost of $3.75 each, another reward for their elite status.

The sharpshooters were used in unconventional ways that were both highly effective and hazardous. Instead of the company-sized formations of conventional units, Berdan's sharpshooters often operated in four-man fire teams or "comrades in battle." Their primary missions were as skirmishers and to provide flank security, rather than the sniper role that their marksmanship skills would imply – although they did a fair amount of sniping, too.

Unlike the conventional forces, the sharpshooters had excellent fire discipline. Normally two men from a cell would work together, alternating their firing. The first man would fire, but the second man waited until the first had reloaded before making his shot, then the procedure was reversed. This insured that at least one loaded weapon was always available to cope with an emergency, and that there was a sustained, deliberate fire against the enemy.

ABOVE *A Confederate soldier waits in earthen breastworks prior to the Battle of the "Mule Shoe" that was a part of the Wilderness Campaign fought May 5–6, 1864. The action took place west of Fredericksburg, Virginia, along the Orange Turnpike and Plank Roads.*

Confederate Sharpshooters
Confederate forces developed and maintained a similar kind of unit, generally known as the Whitworth Sharpshooters. Formed in 1862, within the Army of Tennessee, this unit was tasked with the same kind of flank security, skirmishing, and covering missions as the Union version, and it seems to have performed just as well.

The Rebel snipers specialized in extreme long-range precision fire. Instead of rapid-firing Sharps, though, many of them used imported English Whitworth rifle. This marvelous implement was a .45cal, high-velocity, sturdy weapon imported by the Confederacy from England. The result of some very careful research and development work and precision manufacture, the Whitworth had been designed as a deluxe hunting rifle.

The South managed to import about 150 of these weapons, a few at a time, and issued them typically one to a brigade. Each cost at least $500 in gold, including 1,000 rounds of ammunition, each charge and projectile carefully weighed and packed in little tin trays. This consistency was essential for long-range precision fire.

Each rifle also came equipped with a folding, ladder-type rear sight calibrated to 1,200 yards, and most had an excellent Davidson 4X scope mounted on the left side of the stock. The Whitworth was designed to use a special bullet, the shape of which mated with the hexagonal rifling of the bore. To maintain the accuracy of which the weapon was capable, each round had a carefully weighed bullet (530 grains) backed by 85 grains of specially manufactured black powder packaged in a waxed linen cartridge. The weapon was extremely accurate at long range, but fouled easily and was very slow to load.

Slow or not, the Rebel sharpshooters were nothing short of amazing in their documented ability to engage targets at ranges that challenge modern shooters and modern weapons of the very best kind – 1,000-yard shots were almost routine, while occasional kills were made at ranges of up to a mile.

Pace off 300 yards sometime and take a look at a human being at that range – it is an extremely challenging target, just standing still, and one that is beyond the ability of almost every modern, highly trained soldier. Then double that to 600 yards, and your target will be almost invisible on level terrain. At a measured 1,000 yards, a human being is just a tiny speck, easily masked by the crosshairs of even the Whitworth's 4X scope. Only the best Marine and Army snipers will attempt such a shot today, and then only with specialized .30cal and .50cal rifles equipped with 12X scopes.

Confederate sharpshooters managed to dominate the edges of the battlefield to a degree that their Union counterparts never approached. There were few of them, but as Major General Sedgwick learned the hard way, they could hit almost anything they wanted. If they could see you, they could hit you.

These long-range shots seem virtually impossible today, particularly when you consider the ballistics of those old low-velocity projectiles, the loose powder, low-power optics, lack of precision rangefinders, and the stress of battlefield conditions, but they were well documented, over and over. How do you use a precision weapon and ammunition to best effect?

First, you must know the range to your target with precision, and the farther away the target, the more important the range information. That's because the arc of the trajectory increases with distance: out at 1,000 yards, it will be plunging at a steep angle. If you are off in your range estimation by a hundred yards or so, the bullet may impact in front of or behind the target.

Rebel sharpshooters practiced range estimation constantly. On the march, they'd pick out a landmark along the road, estimate its range, then pace it off while they marched along. If you do that

BELOW *The most effective and efficient killers on the Civil War battlefield were the handful of Confederate soldiers equipped with the amazing Whitworth rifle, all of whom were sudden death out to 1,000 yards.*

a few hundred times, you get to know the difference between the appearance of a man at 900 yards and 1,050 yards quite well.

Second, these Rebel snipers were the best of the best marksmen in the ranks, and the ranks were full of men from the backwoods, where they depended on their rifles for food and protection.

Finally, the Whitworth snipers worked at their craft every day, getting to know the performance of their individual rifles at long range. If you spent all day, every day, estimating range, wind, and slant angle to targets, firing on them, and evaluating your shots, and firing the best weapon on the battlefield, you'd become good at the job, too.

Tactical Use of Sharpshooters

The most common mission for these units was out in front or to the sides of the main force on a march, the classic skirmishing role. Typically, the commander "chopped" two or more companies from a trusted

regiment out front and to the flanks, about 400 yards from the leading element of the main force in open terrain. The men then deployed in skirmisher formation, with a five-yard interval – if they did it by the book.

That provided a screening force about a half-mile long in a big arc, out in front. If they bumped into the opposition and engaged, there was a lot of firepower to cut loose. Their standing orders would have told the skirmishers what to do in the event of contact, depending on the nature of the enemy force – to pull back, stay put, or attack. In any event, the commander of the skirmishers would have sent a runner back to the main force commander with a report.

The Berdan Sharpshooters were masters of the skirmishing role. When in open skirmish formation, they relied on bugle commands to maneuver and control the unit, much of which might have been out of sight of the commander, but not out of hearing.

At that time, sharpshooters didn't use the term "sniper," a British invention of about the same time, but instead called the mission "special service." However, the idea was the same as the concept of the sniper today– a particularly skilled rifleman who can engage targets with precision at extreme range, normally from deep cover and complete concealment.

Although many of the members of the sharpshooter regiments were skilled at very-long-range precision fire, they had learned their craft with heavy bench-rest rifles weighing up to 35 pounds. Superman himself couldn't lug a 35-pound rifle on a march, and neither did these men. The Sharps was perfect for most of the missions they performed, few of which involved extreme long-range shooting.

But occasionally such a mission was assigned and, for the purpose, each company of the US Sharpshooters carried one or two of the heavy match rifles in a supply wagon. Such a weapon would be employed against enemy commanders, gun crews, artillery horses (without which a gun was immobilized), and similar high-priority targets.

The marksman was authorized to operate quite independently, roaming the battlefield looking for new business. Sometimes he would climb a tree for better visibility and cover; other times he would dig a hole or set up a firing position in a house. From such a position, he could engage enemy targets with reasonably good security – most of the time. But occasionally, one sniper would start shooting at another in a long-range duel.

That's what happened to Private John Ide in April 1862, at the siege of Yorktown, Virginia. Ide and a Confederate sniper started banging away at each other across the fortifications, and the Reb scored a direct hit on Ide's head.

There were many such duels throughout the war, and soldiers from both sides sometimes stopped to watch. The truth was that the rank-and-file rather detested the sharpshooters and didn't always mind when one of their own took a hit. That's understandable when you remember that the conventional soldier stood up in battle, in plain sight of the enemy, and took pride in his ability to endure the storm of lead that was directed his way. The work of the skulking sharpshooter, hiding behind trees and walls, and picking off individual soldiers at long range seemed a lot like murder – no matter which side he was on. For many of the troops, there was something dishonorable about the work of the sharpshooters.

Boots and Saddles

ABOVE, RIGHT *Here's the last thing a lot of Union soldiers saw – a Confederate cavalry trooper bearing down on him on 1,200 pounds of agitated horseflesh at about 20 miles an hour, an irresistible force.*

LEFT *The foundation of both armies, North and South, was the common soldier, like this private from the 34th North Carolina Infantry.*

"Who ever saw a dead cavalryman?" the infantry often asked passing cavalrymen, teasing them as soldiers like to do. They were commenting on the cavalry's apparent lack of losses and contact with the enemy, and most seemed to think that a few more dead horsemen might be a good idea. Despite the jests and jibes, a lot of cavalrymen lost their lives during the war, and their bodies were spread across the countryside, not just on the battlefields.

Cavalry is an ancient concept – light, mobile, audacious units used to impose or exploit the element of surprise on the battlefield, to scout, screen, and guard. In ancient times, cavalry units fought on foot; during the Civil War and until World War II, cavalry troopers rode horses; today they use helicopters and light armored vehicles like the Bradley, the Marines' LAV, and the Russians' BMP. Regardless of how a cavalry soldier gets to the fight, the missions are eternal.

Civil War cavalry training, tactics, and employment evolved during the conflict. At first, senior Federal planners and strategists dismissed the need for large cavalry units at all and delayed building a mobile, mounted force. When the Federals finally did get around to creating a cavalry, their tactics wasted the resource, keeping the mounted soldiers under tight rein – until little Phillip Sheridan showed how cavalry should be used.

Actually, the Federals should have known all along how effective cavalry could be: the Confederates were often adept at the art from the very beginning. Rebel cavalry units, particularly in the eastern theater, were often composed of young men of the gentry, who had been taught to ride before they learned to walk.

They were natural horsemen, had excellent, combat-tested leaders, brought their own horses with them, and needed training only in the employment of weapons, not the ability to stay on or care for a horse.

CAVALRY MISSIONS

The cavalry had, and still has, several critical missions within the Army:
• To be the eyes and ears of the force, scouting and patrolling, often at great distance from the main body of troops, engaging the enemy when absolutely necessary – "snoop, scoot, and communicate;"
• Long-range raids and assaults on weakly held enemy depots, transportation facilities, and troop concentrations, using

the elements of surprise and speed;
• Harassment of the enemy's vulnerable flanks and rear, forcing him to redeploy forces away from the main effort;
• To act as a fast, mobile assault force during battle, able to bring combat power to bear with much more speed and potential shock effect than an equivalent number of infantry;
• "Economy of force" missions – attack, defend, delay effectively with fewer resources than an infantry force would require to do the same thing.

BASIC TRAINING FOR THE CAVALRY TROOPER

One reason the Union planners were reluctant to develop a mounted force was the long lead time required to train riders.

MAIN PICTURE *Confederates used their cavalry efficiently and effectively almost from the outset of the war, employing their mounted forces for raids, reconnaissance, screening, "economy of force" missions, and as highly mobile and flexible combat power.*

RIGHT *Although lightly equipped, the Confederate cavalryman was notoriously effective with his saber and carbine, able to move rapidly into advantageous position, deliver accurate and effective fire, then move quickly out of range of a counter-stroke.*

An infantry soldier was lucky to receive a few weeks of instruction. and some went into battle within a week of enlistment. but a competent cavalry soldier – and a competent cavalry horse – took two years to train completely. Many of them were given a month or two instead. and here is what they learned.

HORSES AND HORSEMANSHIP

First. whether they had ridden before or not. troopers learned about horses and horsemanship the Army way. and that begins at the beginning. A horse is a big. somewhat fragile creature with special needs. It is gregarious. emotional. and not always too bright. Once "broken." it will submit to the will of its rider or handler – if it understands what is wanted.

At the beginning of the war. the basic Union cavalry horse was supposed to be 15–15.2 hands high at the shoulder and normally weighed between 900 and 1.000 pounds. It could be any dark color – chestnut. brown. bay. or black.

Despite their size. horses need careful attention to keep them out of trouble. If they eat too much. or drink too much. they get a condition called "colic" and die. If their coats aren't kept clean. they readily suffer from sores. particularly under the saddle. which will put them out of action. They contract respiratory diseases and internal parasites. fight with other horses. and crash into things when they don't look where they're going.

The typical horse doesn't think at all like a human being. but sometimes has all the sense and emotional stability of a three-year-old child. A horse will cry. pout. and make mischief. It may know exactly what you want it to do. and not do it out of spite. Some horses will be affectionate. loyal. and give you the last measure of their devotion: others will kick. bite. and make trouble. A horse has a strong sense of self-preservation and is easily scared. but you can teach most horses to overcome their fear. In fact. almost every horse in

cavalry service would have done your bidding – without rest. without food – until it dropped dead beneath you. And many thousands did just that throughout the war.

General Phil Sheridan. the diminutive and legendary cavalry leader. calculated that the standard GI horse could carry no more than about 250 pounds total if it was to give good service without breaking down. He added up the weight of the

LEFT *Union cavalry soldier bedecked with full field equipment.*
BELOW. LEFT *It takes a long time to train a cavalry horse, but Union forces didn't have a lot of time. Instead, they used quite severe bits to get the mounts to do what was required.*
BELOW *Confederate cavalrymen frequently provided their own mounts and their own tack. These might not have met Union standards, but generally the horses were better schooled and cared for.*

standard McClellan saddle, bridle and tack, the carbine, saber, ammunition, and all the essentials to support the man-and-horse team during extended operations, and it came to about 120 pounds! Subtracting that from the load he knew a standard horse could carry comfortably for an extended period, he came up with his ideal trooper – a man who weighed about 130 pounds and was about five feet six inches tall (the average soldier was only two inches taller back then). While that was Sheridan's ideal, he and the Federal Army took what they could get, and many were a lot larger. The Confederate ideal

was a bit bigger – 155 pounds – and the average trooper in the 9th Virginia Cavalry was five foot eight inches.

Big or small, they had to be strong – each had to be able to place his hands on a horse's withers (the bump at the base of the neck) and mane, and vault up, swinging the right leg over without touching, and gently landing on the horse's back.

The long process of training cavalry troopers began afoot, in what the Army called the "School of the Trooper Dismounted." The neophyte trooper learned all the basics of close-order drill,

then went through the motions for mounted soldiers, but without the mount. In fact, much of his instruction took place on the ground before he tried his new skills mounted.

Part of that instruction covered the saddle, bridle, and basic equipment issued by the Army to the soldier for use on his horse, and for which he was responsible financially. That basic issue included a bridle, a watering bridle, a halter, a McClellan Model 1859 saddle, saddle blanket (blue wool with orange stripe along the edge), surcingle, saddle bags, picket pin and rope, feed bag, curry comb,

brush, and spurs. Each soldier learned how to care for the gear and the horse at the same time.

When they were ready, the men were introduced to their horses. Cavalry basic training taught the new troopers that the horse was always cared for first – starting first thing in the morning, at stable call. The trooper learned to groom his mount with curry comb and brush, to clean its hooves, and to feed and water it. Only when the horse had been cared for could the trooper get breakfast for himself.

After breakfast, they learned the fundamentals of the "School of the Trooper Mounted." Each trooper had to learn the proper way to saddle the horse, the Army way. The saddle blanket was folded three times, forming six layers, with the edges on the left side. The folded blanket was placed gently on the horse's back, then slid to the rear to align the hair, lifted, carried forward, and the process repeated. Next, the saddle was picked up, left hand on the pommel, right on the seat, and carried to the horse, insuring he saw it so as not to be surprised. Each detail of saddling was executed in the specified way, and each trooper was required to demonstrate every skill, by the numbers.

Even such a simple thing as mounting required detailed instruction and practice. You didn't just plop yourself in the saddle – that would have startled and hurt the horse, and it would have been likely to bolt or shy. The new trooper learned to hold the reins in his left hand, maintaining just enough tension to control the horse, place the left foot in the stirrup, and spring up, swinging the leg over, then – gently – lower himself into the saddle. They practiced mounting and dismounting for hours at a time.

THE MILITARY SEAT

Sitting on a horse looks like a simple enough matter, but it isn't, as the troopers quickly learned. The sergeants drilled the soldiers in the proper position of attention, and the proper "seat" – body erect, shoulders back (but not unnaturally), eyes to the front, head up, legs almost in line with the body, balls of the feet on the stirrups, heels about an inch lower. The elbows were held in, close to the body, both hands holding the reins close over the centerline of the horse, above the withers. Troopers were taught, over and over, that their ear, shoulder, hip, and heel should always be in vertical alignment. It was a very different way of sitting on a horse than any of them had done before, in the unlikely event that they had ever ridden at

LEFT *Corporal from the 1st Virginia Cavalry, his saber at the "guard" position.*

all, but when properly carried out, it gave the rider great control, comfort, and mobility.

First, by themselves with a single instructor, the student troopers learned to manage their mounts. Control of a schooled horse is maintained with the rider's weight in the saddle, the pressure and position of the legs, and with the reins. Learning how to manage all these "aids" (as they are called) took time and practice. They rode at the walk, trot, canter, and gallop. They learned that, for an effective charge, all the horses should be aligned in ranks, even at a gallop – and they discovered how extremely difficult that was to accomplish on the drill field, much less on the battlefield.

DRILL, MOUNTED AND DISMOUNTED

When they began to demonstrate control of their mounts, they were drilled in groups – first of three, then more, increasing to platoons, companies, and regiments. Each trooper had to be able to play his part in the maneuvers – moving from column into line, and back again.

Then it was back on the ground to work with weapons – saber, pistol, and carbine. Each weapon has its own problems and possibilities, afoot and on horseback. After learning the basics dismounted, the troopers had to demonstrate proficiency from horseback, firing at a target eight feet high and three feet wide, with a three inch stripe down the middle and a white square in the centre of the stripe.

With the horse standing still, they fired from 10, 20, and up to 50 yards,

ABOVE *Cavalry soldiers might have preferred high boots, but they were issued simple and inexpensive shoes, just like the infantry. These are fitted with standard enlisted soldier's spurs.*

with the target to the left, right, and straight ahead. Then again, at the walk, trot, and gallop. Not only were they scored on target hits, but also the performance of the horse, which was required to maintain its gait and direction, despite the report of the weapons.

Although units were instructed by regulation to supply hay and grain for the horses, the amounts issued were often very inadequate. A horse will graze naturally for 12 hours a day, but military operations didn't permit that. Ideally, grain made up the difference, but grain wasn't always available, particularly to Confederate units.

Instead of 12 or more pounds of oats, corn, or barley – high-calorie food for a horse – the units often had to make do entirely with forage found along the route of march, requisitioned from farmers in the vicinity, or simply stolen. After the sustained operations of both Confederate and Union forces in Virginia, the place had been picked clean and was nearly barren of food for soldier, civilian, and livestock alike. The result was that the horses quickly lost muscle, speed, and stamina. They became sick and often died.

The effect on military operations was tremendous; at some point, the spur stops working and the horse keels over, dead. About a million horses and mules

died during the war. The Union developed an excellent program to provide remounts for cavalry service and was able to replace the losses; Confederate units didn't have such a system and had to scrounge, capture, and scavenge replacement horses, saddles, and equipment – just another form of abrasion in the war that ultimately ground the South into submission.

The cavalry remount system employed detachments of soldiers assigned to prepare mounts for troopers, operating out of a depot near Washington. They supplied horses that, if not fully schooled, at least were healthy and broken to saddle and bridle, and from five to eight years of age. It was up to the troopers to finish their education. Often that happened on combat operations.

Since these horses were very green and unaccustomed to gunfire, they were very difficult to manage when the shooting started. That produced some unhappy incidents. For example, cavalry

doctrine told the trooper to fire over the horse's head, using the head and neck for cover, when engaging a target to the front. During a charge, when the trooper was leaning forward, that put the pistol right between the horse's ears. A typical green horse would rear back when startled like that, and the result could easily leave the trooper with a broken nose.

Even when the trooper didn't receive a broken nose, sometimes he had to fight with his new mount to regain control after each shot. But after a while, if both the trooper and horse survived, they reached an accommodation. The horse became used to the noise, or went deaf, or was so distracted by the overall noise of battle that it didn't notice one more explosion.

COMMAND AND CONTROL OF THE MOUNTED UNIT

The effectiveness and survival of the cavalry soldier and his unit on the battlefield depended very much on everybody "playing off the same sheet of music," working together in a coordinated

ABOVE *Cavalry troopers, particularly Confederates, were adept at fighting dismounted — although they usually used a carbine rather than the rifle shown here. The horse provided rapid mobility from one part of the battlefield to another, or to ambush sites or vulnerable rear areas.*
RIGHT *The saber, when used, could be an effective and fearsome weapon. However, it required tremendous skill and extensive practice. This trooper demonstrates the beginnings of the moulinet, a circular motion of the saber arm while attacking dismounted enemy soldiers.*

way. What we do today with radio and hand-and-arm signals, the troopers of the Civil War did with bugle calls and shouted commands.

The cavalry company could only be maneuvered effectively in combat by bugle calls, so the bugler was required to stay at the side of the company commander. The latter maneuvered the unit by ordering the bugler to sound

"Forward," or "Halt," "To the Left," "To the Right," "The About" (which turned everybody back the other way), "Change Direction to the Left," "Change Direction to the Right," "Trot," "Gallop," "Commence Firing," "Cease Firing," "Charge," and "Rally." Each of these calls was distinctive and every trooper had to learn them, and quickly. Of course, somebody always got it wrong and would go left when he was supposed to go right, halt instead of charge, and go back to the rally point when he was supposed to be going forward. However, the sergeants always found ways of helping such soldiers with their professional education, and the poor lads learned the calls or suffered the consequences.

THE MODEL 1859 McCLELLAN SADDLE

The McClellan saddle was an interesting piece of 19th-century military technology, introduced just before the Civil War after

young Captain George McClellan had studied similar versions in use during the Crimean War. Several variations of his design were tested by US cavalry squadrons patrolling Indian territory, and ultimately it was selected over several other saddles, one of its prime virtues being that it was comparatively inexpensive to produce.

Three sizes were issued, with saddle trees of 11, 11$^1/2$, and 12 inches. Leather straps and rings on the front and rear of the saddle permitted stowage of cargo, while a leather thimble on the right (or "off") side was provided for resting the carbine when mounted. Partly because of its good design – and partly because there were tens of thousands of them in storage after the war – the McClellan saddle stayed in the US Army inventory for many years, with slight variations in the spec, right up until the last horse units were finally retired at the time of World War II.

PACKING FOR COMBAT OPERATIONS

Troopers learned how to roll and strap their blankets and poncho to the front and rear of the McClellan saddle, and how to pack the saddlebags in the official, approved Army way. Generally, the cavalry trooper planned to travel as light as possible, but he still had to pack a lot of gear on the horse, and the McClellan saddle was designed to help stow it all.

On the front of the saddle, attached by three straps, was the trooper's greatcoat. This heavy garment provided protection during cold weather, sometimes served as a blanket, and was so bulky that the trooper had to learn the proper way to fold it early in his instruction. On top of the greatcoat, readily to hand in case of rain, was strapped the rubberized poncho, neatly folded.

On the right side of the horse, at the front of the saddle, was secured the animal's feed bag, a handy device made of double-stitched canvas with a leather base. The mount's grain ration was often carried in this bag, with the top folded over, although on the march it was rarely very full. The feed bag was quite watertight when wet and was handy for collecting water for the horse, and sometimes the rider.

At the rear of the saddle, the trooper attached his saddlebags and strapped down his personal blanket, and perhaps (if he bothered) his shelter half, two tent pins, and the six-foot length of rope used with the tent. Inside the rolled blanket were likely to be any spare clothes the trooper decided to take with him on campaign.

A brass stud and two loops fitted corresponding holes in the skirts of the bags; two leather tabs passed through the loops to secure them. One of the saddlebags contained all the trooper's accessories – extra ammunition, cleaning patches for his weapons, extra hardtack and salt pork for longer operations, and his "lucifers," or matches. A shaving kit and "housewife" (as the sewing kit was called) were standard. The other bag was mostly reserved for the horse: curry comb, brush, hoof pick, rag, and sometimes saddle soap. Both Federal saddlebags had a pocket to stow a spare horseshoe and ten nails.

Although the troopers tried to keep the personal gear and horse gear separated, it was more important to equalize the weight, so sometimes the

LEFT *The McClellan saddle was light, simple, and inexpensive. With minor modifications, it continued to be issued to US Army troopers until the end of World War II.*

contents of the bags became a little mixed.
As the war progressed, the troopers left
more and more behind, and the
saddlebags became flatter and lighter. In
any event, they were quite small and
really couldn't accommodate much more
than the absolute essentials.

Every trooper was issued a picket pin
and a 30-foot rope, called a "lariat" by
the Army. This permitted the horse to be
tethered in a pasture with a reasonably
good chance that he'd be around in the
morning. The lariat was also used to rig a
high picket line for hitching several horses
by their halter ropes. On campaign,
though, the horses were too tired to stray
far and normally were turned loose at
night to feed.

A cavalry trooper carried a haversack
like everybody else, wearing it over the
shoulder in the same way. The haversack
had a muslin lining with little pockets,
intended to separate the sugar, coffee, salt
"horse" (as the salt beef and pork were
often called), and the 20 or 30 blocks of
hardtack commonly issued until cooked.
However, usually the muslin was used as
cleaning patches for the carbine or pistol.
The result was that the trooper's rations
usually became mixed up in a ghastly
mess.

THE SABER

"Draw – SABER!" was the command that
ordered the cavalryman to reach over his
left arm, run his right hand through the
loop of cord called the "sword knot,"
grasp the grip, and withdraw the weapon.
First, it was extended fully, held to the
front and right at a 45-degree angle for a
moment, then brought back to a vertical
position, edge forward, point slightly
above the shoulder, to the position of
Attention.

Early in their training, the troopers
became very well acquainted with the
saber, a much more challenging, and
sometimes more effective, weapon than
the pistol or carbine.

Although both sides tended to favor
the pistol and carbine later in the war, the
saber proved to be a valuable battlefield
weapon, one that is not very well
understood today.

Successful use of the saber demanded
excellent riding skills from the trooper – a
perfect seat, gentle hands, balanced and
supple. When cavalry units were able to

ABOVE, RIGHT *Right side of McClellan
saddle, showing blanket roll, feed bag,
carbine thimble, and rubber blanket.*
RIGHT *Left side of McClellan saddle,
showing lariat, picket pin, and haversack.
The trooper is wearing his greatcoat,
normally folded and rolled, then strapped
to the front of the saddle.*

surprise enemy infantry and attack them before they could react, the saber was marvelously effective.

Here's how they did it. The charge began with the troop or platoon on line in two ranks, at a walk. The platoon leader or sergeant commanding the unit ordered, "Draw – SABER!" Then, "Forward – MARCH!" The unit moved out at a walk, each trooper dressing right and left, insuring the formation was aligned. Then, at the command, "Trot – MARCH!" the pace was increased, alignment being maintained.

Each trooper carried the saber in his right hand, blade upright and in line with the right shoulder, edge to the front. At this stage, he should have had his enemy in sight and begun to select his target. The unit commander ordered the bugler to sound the charge, and the whole line would urge the horses forward, maintaining the line and the interval between horses.

At this point, the enemy had a tremendous tactical problem. The line of horsemen would have been approaching at about 20 miles an hour, closing rapidly. The horses, each weighing over a thousand pounds, would run right over a man if he stood still, and could outrun him unless he was very close to cover. If the enemy were in the open, dispersed, without cover, they could get off one shot at the cavalry – no more. They could dodge left, right, or run away, but all of the choices were very risky. Unless that first and only shot immediately disabled the horse or the rider, there was no time to reload. The bayonet and musket might have been used to parry the rider's saber, but that took more skill than the common soldier usually possessed.

This was where all the practice paid off. The trooper rode right down on his victim, watching to see which way he would break. If he turned and ran directly away, he would simply die tired. The point of the saber kills, the edge of the saber at least wounds. The trooper would try to take the enemy on the horse's right side, then plunge the point of the saber into the upper midsection of the man, withdrawing the point with a rotary movement of the weapon called the "moulinet," as horse and rider thundered past.

If the enemy stood to fight, perhaps waiting to fire until in close range, then attempting to parry the saber with the musket, the well-trained cavalry soldier could easily deflect the blow, on right or left side of the horse, and execute a cut or thrust.

During the whole fight, the trooper always kept his seat, never stood in the stirrups, and never hacked at the enemy soldier with the weapon raised over his

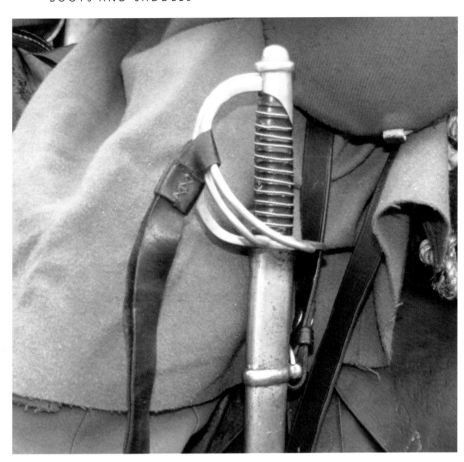

THIS, AND FACING PAGE *The saber is unhooked once the trooper is mounted. When it is needed, the trooper places his right hand through the leather loop called the "sword knot," then he draws the weapon. Normally, when moving into the attack, the saber is carried point up, edge forward, hilt at about waist level.*

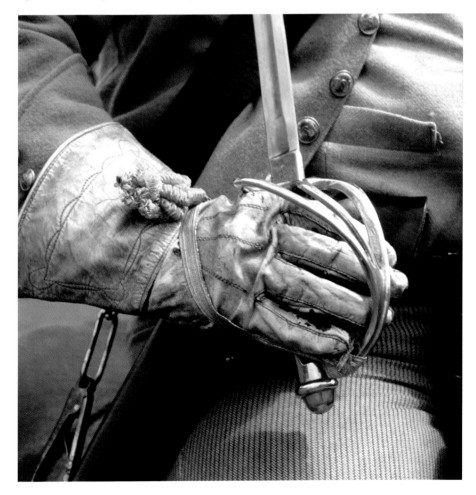

head. He maintained control of the horse with his legs and balance, seldom with the reins.

As the war progressed, soldiers' attitudes toward the weapon changed. After the battle at Shiloh, Confederates in Nathan Bedford Forrest's command were ordered to turn in their sabers, now considered obsolete. For the rest of the war, they carried two pistols and a carbine, and fought mostly dismounted

as dragoons. Others took intense pride in their ability with an edged weapon, sharpened their blades, and built their doctrine around both the saber charge and the dismounted fight with the carbine.

Properly used, the saber produced immediately incapacitating wounds, without a lot of muscular effort from the trooper – the horse's speed and inertia provided the power.

Sabers of many patterns, models, and makes were issued to the troopers of both sides over the course of the war. Of these, though, the Model 1860 Light Saber (and its copies) was probably the most common. It was a handsome weapon, 43 inches long overall, with a pronounced curve to the blade. The saber was somewhat longer than the much straighter sword carried by officers and some sergeants as a badge of office, and, unlike

MAIN PICTURE *Cavalrymen fight at close quarters during the Battle of Cedar Creek in the Shenandoah Valley.*
RIGHT *Confederate cavalry soldiers' tools of the trade.*

the sword, was intended primarily for combat. It weighed about three-and-a-half pounds out of the scabbard, about five-and-a-half pounds when sheathed.

Troopers wore the saber "hooked up" when afoot, otherwise its point would trail on the ground. The sword belt was equipped with a brass hanger for the saber, which was attached in the reversed position, so that it hung with the point forward. This may sound odd, but the reason would become apparent if you tried to walk with one in what seems to be the normal position, point to the rear.

The saber was an extremely difficult weapon to master, for something that appears so simple and brutal. The novice trooper worked with it for hours every day, practicing maneuvers that were both practical and conditioning. The physical conditioning was essential because the saber required that same combination of strength and flexible control that was necessary to ride well, called "suppleness."

The key to developing control and suppleness was a series of saber drills borrowed from French cavalry training and doctrine of the 1850s, an elaborate series of exercises called the "Manual of the Saber." Novice troopers learned the proper way to draw and return the saber, to parry thrusts and cuts from enemy soldiers on horseback as well as on the ground. They practiced by "running at heads" – trying to skewer targets the size and shape of a human head – and at even smaller suspended rings, first at a walk, then a trot, and finally at a gallop.

Even then, military planners understood the need to "train the way you fight," so the drills were intended to make the cavalry trooper react automatically when confronted with a threat, cutting, parrying, or thrusting the saber.

There was a real hazard to the horse when fighting with edged weapons, so the troopers were carefully schooled in all the maneuvers while keeping a safe clearance from their trusty mounts.

THE CARBINE

Particularly at the beginning of the war, troopers employed any firearm available – shotgun, rifle, or carbine. The carbine turned out to be the best choice, and of the carbines, the Sharps New Model 1859 version was especially popular. It was, like its longer infantry version, easy and fast to load, accurate, and hard hitting.

But the Spencer was used extensively, too, and it offered breechloading, lever-action technology of a high order. A .52cal weapon, just 39 inches long and weighing about nine pounds loaded, the Spencer wasn't issued till 1863; even so, it quickly became the most common shoulder-fired model in Union service. Its self-contained ammunition made loading easy in the saddle, and avoided the problems cavalry troopers experienced with the paper cartridges used for the Sharps, which often became smashed in the cartridge boxes as a result of all the bouncing around on horseback.

Unlike the Sharps, the Spencer was a magazine-fed weapon with an eight-round capacity: seven in the magazine, one in

RIGHT *Using his balance and seat as primary aids, the cavalryman guides his horse directly at his victim, who will break to the left or right, or run away. The point of the saber does the killing, and it works well no matter where the enemy tries to escape.*
BELOW *The Sharps carbine was powerful, accurate, and almost "soldier-proof," and was extremely common toward the end of the war.*

ABOVE *Delivering accurate, effective fire with a short-barreled carbine from a moving horse, in the heat of combat, was a challenge. Most Confederate soldiers had the extra difficulty of reloading.*

the chamber. Its fully self-contained copper rim-fire cartridges were stored in tubular, spring-loaded magazines that could be exchanged quickly. About 95,000 Spencer carbines were issued, and by the end of the war, virtually all Union cavalry troopers were using Sharps or Spencer breechloaders.

The Confederates used them when they were "donated" by Union forces, but the rimfire cartridges required sophisticated production techniques that the South couldn't develop, so any captured Spencers would have had to be fed captured ammunition as well.

Many other shoulder weapons were used by the cavalry of North and South, both breech- and muzzle-loading. Early in the war, the long, heavy Colt .56cal revolving rifle was issued to some units, including the 9th Pennsylvania Cavalry in 1862. The problems of this weapon were somewhat extreme, and it was not nearly as popular as the excellent pistol version. It was very difficult to reload on horseback, although some soldiers carried spare, preloaded cylinders and attempted to swap them in action – a sure way to drop the cylinder wedge and make the weapon totally useless. But the real hazard with the Colt rifle was the need for a good seal over each charge in the cylinder, done with a coating of lard or butter on top of the bullet. This prevented the propellant gases from one discharge setting off the charges in adjacent bores in the cylinder.

Normally, the carbine would be attached to a wide leather belt draped across the left shoulder by means of a clip on the sling and a ring on the side of the carbine. This allowed a trooper to drop the weapon while fighting with the saber afoot. So the SOP was that the trooper attached the weapon to the clip before mounting, then draped it over his back as he mounted. Once in the saddle, he inserted the muzzle in its socket on the right side of the saddle. At about the same time, he unhooked the saber and was ready for action.

Carbines, because of their shorter sight radius and shorter barrels, were a little less effective in combat, being accurate to about 200 yards rather than 400. Usually, that wasn't much of a problem, because the cavalry trooper tried to get in close quickly, mix it up with the enemy and get him running, rather than

attempt the kind of deliberate engagement conducted by infantry units.

THE PISTOL

Colt single-action Model 1860 Army and Model 1851 Navy revolvers were the dominant sidearms for cavalry troopers on both sides throughout the war. The Army model was a six-shot percussion weapon in hard-hitting .44cal. The Navy was visually similar, but fired smaller .36cal bullets. Similar Colt pistols had been readily available for ten years prior to the war, and many were in private hands in the south. Copies for Confederate troopers were made in small, but important, quantities by several Southern manufacturers, but the main source of supply took the form of captured weapons from Union soldiers and their stores.

Remington Army and Navy pistols were nearly as common as the Colts, in the same calibers, and were strengthened with the addition of top straps. Many other pistols were carried, too, some using metallic cartridges.

Pistols of all types and calibers received a workout in the Civil War cavalry. The weapons offered good firepower for intermediate-range engagements between the saber's need for extreme close contact and the carbine's single shot. Troopers could use pistols to deal with multiple threats within about ten yards or so – a cluster of infantry, for example, or a group of prisoners under guard. They were good for a cavalry charge, permitting the troopers to engage from farther out than with the saber.

Cavalry troopers often preferred the pistol over the saber, and many started carrying two later in the war, leaving the saber back in camp. As J. E. B. Stuart

ABOVE *The carbine remained strapped to the trooper when he was mounted, but a thimble on the saddle provided support to keep the weapon from flopping around during non-combat operations.*

liked to say, "If you're close enough to stick 'em, you're close enough to shoot 'em," and he was right, although apparently nobody mentioned to Stuart that it wasn't necessary to reload a saber.

CAVALRY, MOUNTED INFANTRY, AND DRAGOONS

Well before the Civil War, in Europe, where war was a growth industry, two kinds of mounted force developed and evolved. One was the horse cavalry, units intended to move quickly around the battlefield and fight from horseback. The

ABOVE *Three very common cavalry carbines (from the top): Sharps, Smith, and Spencer. Each had its virtues, but the Spencer was the first really successful American repeating rifle in military service. All sorts of other weapons were used, including shotguns, full-length muskets, and single-shot muzzle-loading carbines, but these were the preferred weapons of most cavalry troopers.*

other was the "dragoon" formation of light infantry soldiers, who rode instead of walked from one part of the battlefield to another, then dismounted and fought on foot. The two kinds of unit were given quite different kinds of training and equipment, the dragoons receiving much heavier swords together with very sturdy pistols and carbines.

This experience gradually trickled across the Atlantic, leading to the formation of two dragoon regiments for the US Army in the 1830s. The Federal units, the 1st and 2nd Dragoon Regiments, were converted to the 1st and 2nd Cavalry Regiments; the

Mounted Rifles (a mounted infantry unit) became the 3rd Cavalry; and the single Federal cavalry unit then in existence was rechristened the 4th Cavalry.

Regardless of the name, Rebel and Union cavalry units often acted like dragoons and mounted infantry, the Confederates under Forrest making a cult of the role, discarding their sabers, and becoming extremely adept at quick-strike operations. Forrest's men, in particular, were extremely good at searching out Federal supply trains, isolated garrisons, and vulnerable units, then rapidly dismounting and attacking from cover.

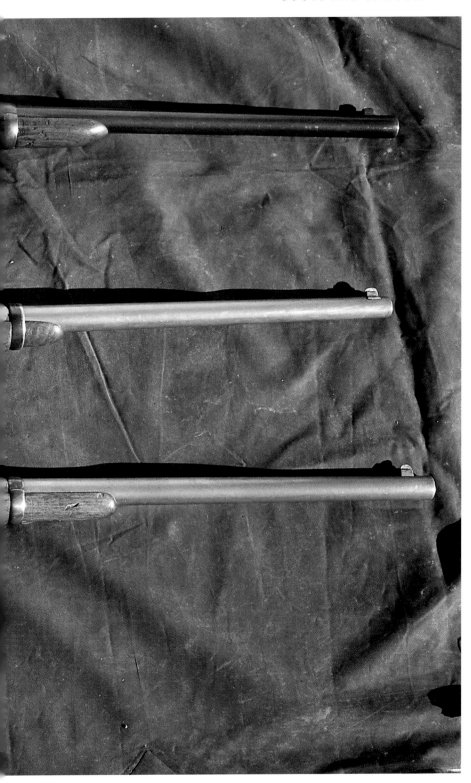

seeking strength in numbers. The Union forces turned around and fought, not knowing what they were facing. Before they could mount an effective counter-attack, the Rebel cavalry dismounted and began to engage with a growing volume of well-aimed and effective rifle fire. Confederate troopers continued to arrive, enlarging the force, and some of them were ordered to attack the Federals' rear and flank. The Federals turned and began an orderly withdrawal.

That's when the Rebels remounted and charged into the retreat, turning it into a rout. The fight became intense, at very close quarters, and the road became littered with dead, wounded, and abandoned equipment.

BASIC CAVALRY TACTICS

While both sides discounted the importance of mobile, mounted units of brigade or larger size at the beginning of the war, the Union in particular neglected their potential. If you had joined the Federal cavalry, perhaps with visions of glory and excitement and a ride in the country, you were not likely to have been happy with your service in 1861 or '62. Although some combat missions were executed during this period, most senior commanders wanted the cavalry used for courier, picket, and escort duties.

These assignments were performed by men in small, scattered commands and required duties the troopers considered mostly loathsome. If, for example, you had been detailed for "vedette" (as a mounted picket is called) duty, you and your horse would have been sent out in advance of the main body of troops, sometimes several miles, to your assigned post. You would have been required to remain mounted, on the alert, for up to six hours at a time, with your carbine out of its socket, ready to engage the first wayward enemy who might stumble into view.

Six hours in a McClellan saddle, not going anywhere, was not comfortable for man or horse. And this vedette duty was performed around the clock, in pouring rain and blazing sun. The troopers hated it. They hated it more when Rebel sympathizers and partisans, known as "bushwhackers," ambushed the pickets, killing them and capturing their valuable weapons, saddle, and tack.

When not on vedette duty, individual troopers were used to carry messages from one commander to another, and to serve as guards and orderlies for senior officers as they moved about the area.

As the war evolved, though, cavalry units grew to brigade and division strength, and they began to be used for independent operations as well as for critical missions in major engagements.

Their speed and well-disciplined fire created a shock effect that went far beyond their apparent combat power – dragoons in everything, but name.

THE CAVALRY IN BATTLE

A good example of that kind of fight, before they abandoned the "long knife," was the experience of the 300 men of Forrest's Tennessee Cavalry Battalion at Sacramento, Kentucky, on December 28, 1861. These troops, mostly inexperienced and unblooded, were conducting a long-range scouting mission when they found the trail of a Union cavalry force. Without

really knowing what they were getting into, and after a patrol that had already covered 20 miles that day, the bugler sounded the gallop, and off they went down the road. About 20 minutes later, the lead elements of the battalion caught up with the Federals' rear guard. After a dash like that, the battalion was spread out along the route of march, but the point element attacked anyway.

That kind of brash assault, particularly on a rear guard, will create panic and disorder in most units, and that's what happened. The rear guard quickly fell back on the main body,

The 4th Virginia Cavalry at "Portici" where General J. E. B. Stuart's cavalry fought Union General John Bufford's troops on August 30, 1862, during the Battle of Second Manassas.

ABOVE *Many makes and models of pistol were used by Civil War cavalry troopers, the Colt Navy, in .31 inch caliber, and this Colt Army, in .44 inch caliber, filled the holsters of most troopers on both sides of the war.*

LEFT *The Sharps carbine was the most successful cavalry weapon of the war – easily reloaded in the saddle, powerful, accurate, and reliable. Confederate troopers used captured Sharps whenever possible.*

The fundamental technique used by cavalry units to close with and destroy their enemy at the beginning of the war was the charge, executed at a pace even faster than the gallop. The charge might have been carried out in one of three variations: on line, in column, or as foragers.

The bugle call "Charge on Line" brought an entire squadron (two cavalry companies) into line, one or two ranks deep, then against the enemy across a wide front. This required terrain and circumstances that allowed the squadron to deploy itself unobserved – a difficult trick. When the squadron moved to the attack from the column, as, for example, when the lead element stumbled onto a suitable opportunity and the whole command was strung out along a road, the bugler ordered the charge and the unit responded by attacking in sequence, front to rear.

Alternatively, the squadron could have executed "Charge as Foragers." For this command, the troopers were spread out randomly, rather than on line or in column, and on command engaged targets of their own selection.

One such assignment could have been the capture of an enemy artillery battery. Typically, a unit would have been ordered into line of battle, two ranks deep, out of range of the enemy guns, and the order to draw sabers would be given. The bugler sounded the call for "Charge on Line," the sergeant or lieutenant pointed his saber toward the objective, and ordered, "CHARGE!"

If you had been a Civil War cavalry soldier at that moment, here's what it might have been like: Horses like to run, so unless your mount is weary from a long march, or frightened by all the noise, he's likely to take off at a gallop. It's important to maintain alignment in the charge, as much as the ground permits, so you need to speed him forward or hold him back in line with the other horses.

This becomes more difficult as you get closer. Of course, the enemy battery will shift its fire to your unit when the gunners become aware of the attack and as you come in range. Their first rounds will be solid shot or shell, and if the gunners know their business, even these will start grinding away at your assaulting force.

The solid shot will easily rip apart any man or animal it hits, even at a mile. And the six guns in the battery will be able to get off many shots into your ranks during the attack. If the horses are green remounts, they will be extremely difficult to manage – they will balk and buck and maybe run away. George Armstrong Custer's horse ran away during one battle and hid in a ditch, with the future general aboard – swearing, spurring, and whipping the horse in an effort to get him under control.

If the gun crews are good at their business and the fuses are cut correctly, the shells will start exploding in and around your ranks. The shell fragments will go whizzing past, perhaps hitting the man next to you, or his horse, or your own.

Even so, there is something electric about an assault, if the casualties aren't too heavy. You are saturated in adrenaline and probably are without fear. The inertia of the charge carries all its survivors along, covering the ground quickly, closing on the enemy battery.

At about 300 yards or so, the battery will change to canister rounds. If the guns are 12-pounders, each canister round will contain 27 iron balls one-and-a-half inches in diameter. They will fire single, then double canister at you, each iron ball a deadly little cannonball in its own right, far more lethal than a bullet. The effect is like firing a huge shotgun into a crowd, cutting wide swaths in the ranks of your unit.

If you are lucky enough to survive this storm of iron, the objective is only seconds away. The gunners' fortitude is now being tested. Some will be ready to run, others steady and standing fast. Rather like kamikaze pilots, the survivors of this impetuous assault crash down on the gunners, some trying frantically to serve the guns, while others abandon the enterprise and try to flee.

Now your saber goes to work. There is a tremendous difference between training for combat and combat itself, so if this is your first time using the weapon against living people, the experience may come as a shock. If you've been trained well, you should function pretty much automatically – an enemy gunner appears, you urge your horse at him. He raises his musket with its bayonet to block your saber – you parry the move instinctively with the blade, then execute a cut toward his head as you bear in on him. The blade catches the soldier just above the collar, the horse's motion carrying you and the saber forward, the blade carving into his neck, about three inches deep. The tendons and muscles holding the head erect are severed almost instantly, along with the jugular artery. He makes a loud, squealing screaming wail,

knowing he has been killed, but will have to wait a little while to bleed to death. You may find the experience horrific, or somehow pleasing, or it may not affect you at all.

ABOVE *Cavalry troopers became expert in traveling light and getting along with the minimum of gear.*

LIFE IN THE SADDLE

During the course of the Civil War, cavalry weapons, tactics, and practice changed tremendously. From small, company-sized units at the outset – assigned to trivial and inconsequential duties – cavalry forces grew to division and corps size, 12,000 men strong. These

LEFT *Dale McCabe depicts General J. E. B. Stuart leading a charge against Federal forces.*

big units could function as independent, highly effective task forces.

Equipped with their own integral "flying" artillery, able to move at the same fast, sustained pace, these massive cavalry units changed the battle and the battlefield. By the end of the war, Union cavalry under Sheridan was conducting highly coordinated operations with the slower foot soldiers, seeking out Confederate units, holding them at bay, and summoning the big infantry corps to come up and finish the job. That is how the Army of Northern Virginia was finally ground down and cornered in April 1865, at Appomattox Court House, and Lee forced to surrender.

The cavalry soldier evolved, too. He joined the cavalry at the beginning of the war to be part of a dashing, romantic kind of service, and was considered to be much more elite than the common foot soldier of the infantry regiments. But he learned that, in some ways, cavalry service was even more dangerous and exhausting.

A trooper was responsible for the care of his horse first, then himself, every day. At the end of the day, the trooper had to find forage for his mount before making supper for himself. That could involve hours of searching for hay or grain.

Instead of being a dashing, romantic ride in the country, cavalry service was a bloody, exhausting business. Even the infantry usually had logistics support from wagon trains loaded with food for men and animals; the infantry received mail, its wounded went to hospitals. The cavalry trooper lived off the land, and the people alongside the road. When he was wounded too badly to ride, he was abandoned to the dubious mercies of his enemies.

More often than the infantry, the troopers dropped by the side of the road to sleep in the mud, so tired that nothing would keep them awake. They fell asleep in the saddle, slumped over their rolled greatcoats, even falling out of the saddle, asleep.

Troopers often ate their salt pork raw, simply because they didn't have time to cook it, or couldn't risk a fire, or just couldn't manage to find anything that would burn. When they could risk a fire and had time, they made coffee immediately, just like the infantry. They ate blackberries when they could find them, and would beg, borrow, requisition, and steal any chickens, hams, and bacon – on or off the hoof – and anything else they could find to feed themselves.

LESSONS LEARNED

Cavalry troopers modified the way they armed and equipped themselves, based on the experience of sustained operations.

The breechloaders allowed much higher rates of fire than the simple muzzle-loaders, so Union troopers, in particular, began carrying much more ammunition. They removed the wooden blocks in the cartridge boxes, designed to store just 20 rounds. With the blocks gone, the boxes would hold 40–60 cartridges. And the troopers learned that, left loose, the cartridges would break apart, so they kept them in the packets of ten rounds, as issued. It took a little longer to break open these packages, but the ammunition was usable instead of a mess of loose powder and bullets. Instead of the 40 rounds normally available to troopers going into action early in the war, after Gettysburg, the cavalry soldier would have at least 140 rounds in his box and saddlebags, and might even carry a second cartridge box attached to the carbine sling with up to 60 more rounds.

Some units and individuals started putting the saber on the saddle, rather than on the sword belt. It wasn't useful dismounted, and was in the way, so leaving it with the horse made a lot of sense when the soldiers were fighting on foot.

CAVALRY FIGHT AT BRANDY STATION, VIRGINIA

Until the fight at Brandy Station, on June 9, 1863, Union cavalrymen were widely considered inferior to Confederate mounted forces, but this engagement changed that. At the end of the battle, J. E. B. Stuart's forces had lost over 500 men, including more than half of the 4th Virginia, although the Rebels still held the field. Here is one Federal cavalryman's letter describing the event:

We were lying at Warrenton Junction, making ourselves as comfortable as possible ... when, on the morning of the 8th of June, 1863, the whole division was ordered out in the lightest of marching order. That night we lay close to Kelly's Ford in column of battalions, the men holding their horses as they slept, no fires being lighted.

At four o'clock in the morning of the 9th, we were again in motion, and got across the ford without interruption or discovery. Yorke, with the third squadron, was in the advance, and ... bagged every picket on the road. Thus, we got almost upon the rebel camp before we were discovered.

We rode right into Jones' brigade, the 1st New Jersey and 1st Pennsylvania

charging together; and before they recovered from the alarm, we had 150 prisoners. The rebels were then forming on the hillside by the station and they had a battery playing upon us like fun. Martin's New York battery then galloped into position and began to answer them.

Our boys went in splendidly, making straight for the battery on the hill. Wyndham himself rode on the right, and Broderick charged more toward the left, and with a yell, we were on them.

We were only 280 strong, and in front of us was White's [Rebel] battalion of 500. As we dashed fiercely into them, saber in hand, they broke ... and over and through them we rode, sabering as we went. By Jove, sir, that was a charge!

[The 12th Virginia Cavalry] came up in support of the rebels, looking splendid, steadier than we did ourselves after the first charge. There was Broderick, looking full of fight, his blue eyes in a blaze and his saber clinched, riding well in front.

At them we went again; I saw Broderick's saber go through a man, and the rebel made a convulsive leap out of his saddle, falling senseless to the

ground. It seemed but an instant before the rebels were scattered in every direction, trying now and then to rally in small parties

Now there were the guns plain before us, the drivers yelling at their horses, and trying to limber up. We caught one gun before they could move it, and were dashing after the others, when I heard Broderick shouting in a stormy voice. The fragments of White's battalion had gathered toward the left of the field, and were charging in our rear.

At the same time, two fresh [enemy] regiments, the 11th Virginia and another, were coming down on our front. The 1st Maryland wavered and broke, and then we were charged at the same time front and rear. We had to let the guns go, gather ourselves together as well as possible to cut our way out.

Gallantly our fellows met the attack. We were broken, of course, by the mere weight of the attacking force, but breaking them up, too, the whole field was covered with small squads of fighting men.

I saw Col. Broderick ride in with a cheer and open a way for the men. His horse went down, but Wood – the bugler

Although they really liked to travel as light as possible, some troopers added a "gum" blanket or small waterproof tarp to their basic load. This, and the standard rubberized poncho, kept the trooper from sleeping directly on the wet ground. In addition, the two items could be rigged over the standard-issue 0-foot lariat to make a small rain-resistant shelter. They could also be used to keep the horse somewhat warmer and drier in bad weather, at the expense of the trooper himself.

Each trooper had a personal blanket as well as the saddle blanket under the saddle on the march. This helped keep the mount's back in good condition and provided the trooper with an adequate bedroll during most of the year. Rebel cavalry troopers seldom had access to the heavy wool saddle blankets used by the Federals and had to make do with normal bedding or makeshifts made from moss.

Another way cavalry soldiers adapted was to discard all spare clothing, with the possible exception of spare socks and one

RIGHT *Captain Thomas E. Williams, 5th United States Regulars, commander of a Union cavalry unit.*

of Company G – gave him his animal, setting off to find another.

Lucas, Hobensack, Brooks, and Beekman charged with twelve men into White's battalion. Fighting hand to hand, they cut their way through, but left nine of the men on the ground behind them. Hughes was left almost alone in a crowd, but brought himself and the men with him safe through. Major Shelmire was last seen lying across the dead body of a rebel cavalryman.

None of us thought anything of two-to-one odds, as long as we had a chance to ride at them. It was only when we got so entangled that we had to fight hand to hand that their numbers told heavily.

I saw all this as a man sees things at such times, in the midst of such confusion, and caught things by passing glimpses. You see, I was myself having as much as I could do... Two fellows put at me. The first one fired and missed. Before he could cock his revolver I succeeded in closing with him. My saber took him just in the neck, and must have cut the jugular. The blood gushed out in a black-looking stream; he gave a horrible yell and fell over the side of his horse, which galloped away.

Then I gathered up my reins, spurred my horse, and went at the other one. As I drove in the spurs it gave a leap high in the air. That plunge saved my life. The rebel had steady aim at me; but the ball went through the horse's brain. His feet never touched the ground again. With a terrible convulsion, the horse turned over in the air, and fell on his head and side, stone dead, pitching me twenty feet.

I alighted on my pistol, the butt forcing itself far into my side; my saber sprung out of my hand, and I lay with arms and legs all abroad, stretched out like a dead man. Everybody had something else to do than attend to me and there I lay where I had fallen.

It seemed to have been an age before I began to come to myself. Every nerve was shaking. There was a terrible pain in my head and a numbness in my side which was even worse. Fighting was still going on around me, and my first impulse was to get hold of my sword. I crawled to it, and sank down as I grasped it once more. I was now able to stand and walk, so holding my pistol in one hand and my saber in the other, I made my way across the fields to where

our battery was posted, scaring some with my pistol and shooting others. Nobody managed to hit me through the whole fight.

Just at that moment, White's battalion and some other [Rebel] troops came charging at the battery. The squadron of the 1st Maryland, who were supporting it, met the charge as well as their numbers went, but were, of course, flanked on both sides by the heavy odds. All of our men who were free came swarming up the hill, and the cavalry were fighting over and around the guns

In spite of the confusion, and while their comrades at the same piece were being sabered, the men at that battery kept to their duty. They did not even look up or around, but kept up their fire with unwavering steadiness. There was one rebel, on a splendid horse, who sabered three gunners while I was chasing him. He wheeled in and out – would dart away and then come sweeping back and cut down another man in a manner that seemed almost supernatural. We at last succeeded in driving him away, but we could not catch or shoot him, and he got off without a scratch.

change of underwear. Many, though, didn't bother with any spares at all. They simply wore their uniforms till they literally fell apart, despite the double layer of fabric on the trousers.

Part of the problem with the trousers came from the McClellan saddle. The constant exposure to rain and frequent lack of saddle soap and leather conditioning oils rotted the seams, allowing the rawhide covering the saddle tree to peel and curl upward like a rough knife. This abraded the clothing of the trooper, and the trooper himself sometimes.

Troopers learned the need to care for their mounts from hard experience; most horses in the war died from neglect, not battle, and the next most common cause was malnutrition. If horses were permitted to stand in mud for long periods during

winter camp, their hooves became diseased, and the animals had to be killed. Some companies only provided one or two brushes and curry combs for the entire complement of mounts, 30–50 horses, with the predictable result that many animals developed skin diseases.

How successful was the cavalry in the Civil War? Sherman remarked, "I have not seen in this war a cavalry command of 1,000 that was not afraid of the sight of a dozen infantry bayonets." But then, the Northern cavalry was substantially worse than its Confederate counterparts until well into 1863. Essential for reconnoitering positions, for screening operations, and skirmishing, the cavalry could not counter the infantry's weight of fire. It could exploit success but rarely was instrumental in achieving victory in set-piece battles.

BELOW *"If you're close enough to stick 'em, you're close enough to shoot 'em," Confederate General Nathan Bedford Forrest liked to say to troopers who wanted to use the saber. The pistol had a longer reach, giving the trooper a bit more "stand-off" distance.*

Artillery, the King of Battle

ABOVE, RIGHT *Company B, 35th Artillery Regiment, 6th Pennsylvania Light Artillery under the command of Captain Burton Baker. The crew uses a ramrod to drive home the cannonball fired by the 5-pound James cannon.*

Of the three main arms of service during the war, the artillery was the smallest, but in many ways the most elite. "Red-legs" (as the Union artillerymen were known, for the distinctive red stripe on their pant legs) needed to be good at math, cool in battle, and team players much more than infantry or cavalry soldiers on either side.

While some artillery units served huge, essentially immobile guns behind established fortifications – the Heavy Artillery (technically, the Foot Artillery) – most of the fighting, killing, and dying was done by the highly mobile Field Artillery.

Both sides used the same basic SOPs for organization and battle, a book called *The Artillerist's Manual*, published in 1863 by Brigadier General John Gibbon, US Volunteers – and both sides modified the standards to suit their resources and responsibilities. Gibbon was one of those rare birds in the early part of the war, a trained soldier who knew his business. He began the war as a captain in the 4th Artillery out west, at Fort Leavenworth, Kansas, and was rapidly promoted, first to chief of artillery for General Irvin McDowell, then to brigadier general and commander of the fabled Iron Brigade, and again to command the 2nd Division, I Corps.

Field artillery had its own organization, but operated as part of what we would call "task forces" or "combat teams" today, with its resources being attached temporarily to larger units.

THE ARTILLERY ARSENAL

Many types and sizes of tube artillery were tried during the Civil War, from primitive six-pounders from the Mexican War to complex and advanced Whitworth breechloaders imported from England. Like the infantry's muskets, the guns came in a rich variety of useful and useless types – rifled and smoothbore, made of bronze, cast iron, and wrought iron. Nearly all were muzzle-loaders. They fired solid shot, shells of several shapes, canister, and grapeshot. The smoothbores were known by the weight of their spherical shot – typically 6- or 12-pounders, while the rifles were described by their bore.It was an exciting time to be in artillery, in more ways than one; tactics and technology

evolved rapidly. However, a few basic types did most of the shooting and killing.

The Legendary Napoleon

One favorite of "red-legs" on both sides was the Model 1857 12-pound field gun, a bronze cannon produced in large numbers, and a common weapon on almost every battlefield. Known informally as the Napoleon, the gun was a reliable, accurate, durable, and easily-

worked weapon, able to engage point targets at ranges of up to a mile. With a bore diameter of 4.62 inches, its solid shot, shell, and canister projectiles were big enough to do considerable damage at short range or long. Standard solid shot backed with two-and-a-half pounds of powder, and with the tube elevated five degrees, would impact on a target 1,619 yards away. Variants of the gun were made by both Union and Confederate

BELOW *A battery of Union heavy artillery with their big guns and white gloves. Units in garrison are traditionally tormented with such affectations, particularly when the enemy is out of sight and mind, but the gloves come off when the fight begins.*

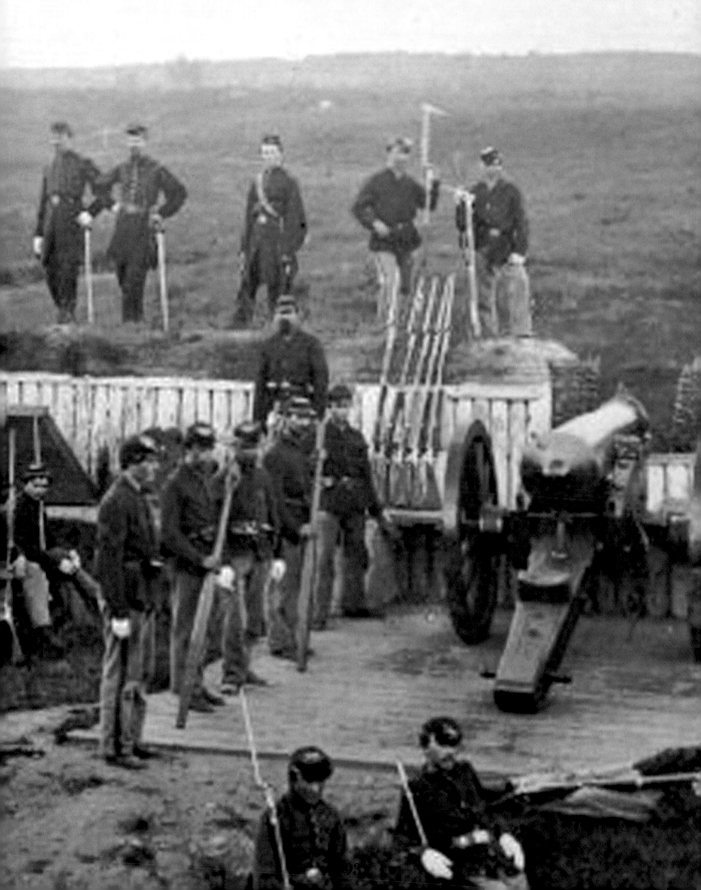

THE FIRST FATAL SHOT

However indifferent men become to human life, they have the most vivid and minute memory of the first man they brought down with deliberate aim. In the instant of time preceding the fatal shot, the features, color of eyes and hair, and even the facial expression are all engraved indelibly on the brain.

"My first man," said an artilleryman, "I saw but twenty seconds; but I shall remember him forever. I was standing by my gun, when a rebel infantry soldier rushed up and made a lunge with his bayonet at one of the horses. I whipped out my revolver and took him through the breast. He tossed up his arms, gave me the strangest look in the world, and fell forward upon his face. He had blue eyes, brown, curling hair, a dark mustache, and a handsome face. I thought, the instant I shot him, that I should have loved that man if I had known him. I tell you what, this war is a terrible business."

arsenals. Despite its smooth bore and heavy tube (1,227 pounds), the 12-pounder had an excellent reputation for accuracy within its effective range, could be reloaded quickly, and when used with canister, maintained a much more effective shot pattern than the Parrott field rifles. Both sides considered the 12-pounder to be the workhorse of the artillery service.

Three-inch Ordnance Rifle

Another favorite in Federal service, and in Confederate, too, when the Rebels could capture them, was the Three-inch Ordnance Rifle. This rifled cannon fired "bolts" (elongated solid projectiles) and shells with great accuracy to long range. The standard charge was only a pound of powder, and with five degrees of elevation, the weapon would throw its projectile a full mile. This gun weighed about 400 pounds less than the Napoleon, 816 pounds for the tube alone, making it somewhat more maneuverable and transportable. At Gettysburg, 146 of them were used by Union forces.

Parrot Rifles

The Parrott Field Rifle was yet another common design on the Civil War

battlefield. Available in 10-, 20-, and 30-pounder designations (and in much heavier sea/coast models), these rifled cannon were generally inferior to the Three-inch Ordnance Rifle, but were used in large numbers anyway. Made of cast iron with a wrought-iron reinforcing band, the Parrott was supposed to be able to withstand high internal pressure. While it is true that the breech seldom failed on these guns, the tubes came apart just forward of the reinforcing band so often that assignment to a Parrott gun crew was sometimes considered defensible grounds for desertion.

SERVING THE GUNS

The fundamental building block of the artillery is the gun and its crew. The care and feeding of the gun is an art and a science, and gun crews became tremendously skilled and efficient at serving their pieces.

A typical cannon was the 12-pounder Napoleon, a smoothbore bronze weapon with a range of a little over a mile and the ability to deliver a wide variety of projectiles. The gun itself rolled on a sturdy carriage, complete with the ancillary tools of the trade. Behind the gun on the firing line would always be

found its limber, a rolling chest with the gun's ready ammunition supply of 50 rounds, their fuses, and primers. Even farther behind the gun would be a caisson containing another 150 rounds.

A standard gun crew comprised eight men in two teams, all supervised by one sergeant, the "chief of the piece." Under his control were three major pieces of mobile equipment, about 12 horses, and seven cannoners. The first team of five men worked the gun itself, under the control and supervision of a corporal. The second team provided the ammunition for the gun from the limber and caisson, also under the supervision of a corporal who, in addition, managed the six drivers.

These men were identified, in good military tradition, by number:

Number One stood by the muzzle, operated the rammer and the sponge. His work was simple, but had to be done with great speed and precision. He pushed the round down the tube, seating it firmly. After the gun was fired, he normally stepped back in front of the muzzle, reversed the rammer, and used the sponge to wash out the bore. This doused any remaining embers in the tube and helped cool it.

ABOVE, LEFT, AND ABOVE Union artillery fire at the Confederate line at Sailor's Creek, Virginia. The cannon crew hoses down the barrel to cool their weapon, uses a coil to clear out any smoldering remains from the previous shot, and loads powder and cannonball. Trained crews could prepare and fire the weapon in very short order – an important skill, since artillery pieces were considered prize targets during the conflict.

BELOW A Napoleon captured from the Confederates is paraded back to Butterfield's Brigade, the Union regiment responsible for its capture near Hanover Court House.

ABOVE *Over a million Union horses and mules died or were killed during the conflict.*
LEFT *The noise of battle frightened many horses, sometimes making them uncontrollable. A huge number of teamsters was required to manage the animals of both armies.*

Number Six was in charge of the limber and its contents. He cut the fuses and used a ballistics table to call out the proper elevation after the Gunner had provided the range to the target.

Number Seven assisted Number Six with the preparation of the ammunition.

Number Eight, when there was one, and the second corporal crewed the caisson, using its ammunition first, then sending it back to the ammo dump for more.

ARTILLERY HORSES

A great deal of the effectiveness of an artillery battery depended on the quantity and quality of its horses, so artillerymen spent a lot of time attending to them before the battle. Without plenty of good feed, grooming, and hoof care, the mobility of the battery was endangered.

Each horse was supposed to be given 14 pounds of hay and 12 pounds of grain (corn, oats, or barley) every day. Multiply that requirement by the hundred or so animals supporting the battery and you have a huge logistics problem. Providing all that grain and hay required teamsters and wagons, and added to the complexity of the problems of the officers and soldiers.

Although a healthy horse can pull a 3,000-pound load over a hard, smooth

Number Two stood on the left side of the muzzle. His primary job was to insert the ammunition into the muzzle.

Number Three stood at the right rear of the piece. During the loading process, he covered the vent with his thumb (protected from the sometimes extreme heat of the tube by a leather thumbstall or glove).

Number Four fired the piece. On command, he inserted the friction primer

in the vent and attached the firing lanyard. On command again, he pulled the lanyard, firing the charge.

The Gunner was at the rear of the tube. From there, he supervised the crew and sighted the gun. When the piece was ready to fire, he – along with the others – stepped aside, out of the path of the recoiling gun.

Number Five delivered each prepared round from the limber to the muzzle.

ABOVE *An artillery sergeant carefully sights an ordnance rifle.*

RIGHT *A very common weapon during the war, the Three-inch Ordnance Rifle could deliver shells and solid "bolts" with precision to targets a mile away.*

road, Civil War artillery horses were expected to pull only 700, partly because of the difficult terrain in which they often moved and partly in anticipation of the large, inevitable losses.

Batteries lost horses by the dozen, in and out of battle. When they died or had to be killed while the battery was in camp, the chore of disposing of the carcasses was a major and generally unpleasant exercise. The typical artillery horse weighed at least 1,200 pounds, and when dead became an awkward package to dispose of. If the expired horse had been allowed to "ripen" for a day or two, the job was notoriously awful, the stench nauseating. Even so, a detail of men assigned to fatigue duty would have to dig a pit big enough, and that was a very big hole in the ground. The legs, stiffened in death, seldom cooperated. Almost 900 horses belonging to Union forces alone died during the three days of battle at Gettysburg, but the armies moved along without bothering to dispose of them.

"CANN-ONNN-EEEEERS – POST!"

So what was it like to be on a gun crew in action? Very exciting and dangerous in battle. The process might begin with a slow, deliberate occupation of positions in anticipation of battle, or the battery might be thrown into action after a long, hard, fast road march.

The Battery Commander

The battery's position on the battlefield would be specified by the regimental or brigade commander, but then it was up to the battery commander, a lowly captain, to decide his "priorities of fire" and targets. This was not usually a problem – Civil War artillery almost always engaged in "direct fire" missions, where the gunners had "eyes on" their target and very rarely conducted indirect fire missions against targets on reverse slopes or otherwise out of sight. Normally, the

first priority would be any enemy artillery battery in range. Second would be high-payoff point targets, like enemy headquarters or assembly areas, if they could be seen. These included houses where enemy commanders and staff were – or might be – meeting, the usual giveaway being all the saddled horses tied up nearby.

Next came any enemy infantry units from about 400 yards out to maximum effective range, about 1,000 yards. Within 400 yards, the immediate threat of

97

attacking infantry made them the first priority. No matter what was happening out there, the battery commander identified the targets, sited the guns, and controlled the fire missions.

Section Chiefs

In theory, each Union battery was expected to have three sections of two guns, although this varied tremendously. Both Union and Confederate batteries often had only four guns. Regardless of how big the battery, each pair of guns was commanded by an officer – the first section by the battery commander, the second by the executive officer, and the third (if there was one) by a lieutenant.

Each section chief supervised and directed the gun crews by designating targets to each of the two gun sergeants in the section.

Gun Sergeants

Each gun sergeant supervised the gun, the limber, and the caisson. He would position his gun, call out the target, and control the rate of fire. The commander, section chiefs, and gun sergeants would put the battery in its battle position, but then it was up to the corporals and privates.

"Action Front!"

When the battery went into action, it would hear a bugle command – "Forward at a Trot," or "Forward at a Gallop," depending on the urgency of the situation, and go hustling along a road or trail, in column. Each Union gun crew should have had 12 horses – the first six pulling the gun and limber with its ready ammunition, the second with another limber and a caisson. Rebel crews had to make do with four horses each. When one of the full-up Union batteries rolled up and went to work, it was quite a sight – as many as 170 men (including all the support personnel) and 98 horses, all in carefully choreographed action. The gun sections each received the order to orient their guns to target areas specified by the battery commander, who would yell,

"Action front!" (or "left" or "right") so the gun sergeants knew how to orient the tubes.

The first section peeled off and occupied its position on the right of the battery, the second section went straight ahead, and the third section moved quickly to the left. Each section's Number One gun moved to the right of Number Two, stopping with the tubes on line and the wheel hubs normally a regulation 14 yards apart.

Since the guns were towed with the muzzles to the rear, maneuvering into position required a big turn, accomplished by much shouting, swearing, and horse sweat. Federal cannoners in field artillery batteries rode the limbers and caissons. In light, or "flying," batteries, everybody had a horse. Rebel gunners, with their four-horse teams, walked into battle.

Even before the guns stopped in position, the cannoners would be running up, taking their own stations. As soon as the wheels stopped turning, the guns were unhooked from the limber. The whole routine was practiced frequently in camp until it all became automatic.

While the gun crews took up their firing positions, the caissons with their extra ammunition, the battery wagon, and the rest of the men set up shop well behind the guns, under cover and protected from most of the inevitable

INSET LEFT *The vent is covered by Number Three, while Number One rams the round home.*

MAIN PICTURE *FIRE! A smart tug on the lanyard fires the charge and sends the projectile screaming downrange.*

INSET BELOW *The workhorse of Civil War tube artillery was the 12-pounder Napoleon field gun, a smoothbore weapon with a bore diameter of slightly over 4½ inches. The only time they were likely to be this shiny was when they were in garrison, or when they were new.*

return fire that would be directed at the battery by the enemy.

Once the battery was in position, the commander identified the targets he wanted destroyed in a way that seems very casual today, and might involve him pointing his saber at a farmhouse in use by the enemy and saying, "Engage that farmhouse on the hill opposite!" He might give all the sections the same target, or assign targets to the sections individually.

Each gun sergeant engaged the target as he saw fit, calling for the type of ammunition he thought appropriate, aiming the weapon, and issuing the command to fire. He also evaluated the fall of the shot and the corrections required – quite a problem with all the smoke on the battlefield.

The appearance of the battery on the battlefield immediately made it a priority target for every opposing weapon system in range. Enemy riflemen may have stopped shooting at infantry targets and begun to engage the battery, even at long range. But enemy artillery and cavalry were the real threats. Counter-battery fire and artillery duels were extremely common during the Civil War and sometimes proved very hazardous.

When that happened, the cannoners received a dose of their own medicine. The cannon of the day were quite capable of shooting ten- or 12-foot shot groups at 1,000 yards or so. That meant that a skilled gun crew and a gunner with a good eye had a pretty good chance of hitting an enemy gun, or its limber or caisson, with the very first shot at that rather close range. A more typical engagement range of 1,500 yards or so might require a few shots to score a hit, but the effect of a good shot would be devastating.

If the gunner really knew his business and had the whole enemy gun section in sight, he'd try for the limber or caisson

ABOVE *Captain R. A. Carpenter led Crenshaw's Battery under the Army of Northern Virginia. This unit was formed and led by officers in Richmond, Virginia. Captain Carpenter poses next to a weapon on display at the battlefield at New Market, Virginia, in the Shenandoah Valley.*
LEFT *A Federal artillery sergeant's insignia of rank.*

first, with shell, solid shot or a bolt; either target would probably blow up on impact, leaving the gun without ammunition and probably creating havoc among the horses and men at the same time. If those targets were masked, he might aim for the horses, perhaps with case or solid shot, or maybe a shell; with the horses dead, the gun couldn't be moved.

Veteran gun crews were notoriously cool in battle. They learned to serve the guns, no matter what. Often they didn't have any weapons for personal defense, the cannon alone providing salvation. When one of the crew dropped, the rest took over his responsibilities, and probably asked him to crawl out of the way if he was still mobile. Crews practiced serving the guns

with as many as six of the eight men out of action; the rate of fire was much slower, but they learned how to do it, and executed it in action – sometimes one man did the whole job by himself, when things got really bad.

THE EFFECT OF ARTILLERY FIRE

No matter what the target, the effect of well-directed artillery fire can be amazing. During the Civil War (and even today), you could actually watch a projectile fly downrange toward its target, a black dot momentarily visible against the sky.

For a soldier between the gun and the target, the experience was different; the projectile was invisible, but produced a loud and highly distinctive sound as it arced overhead – an odd buzzing, for example, like a huge insect, that rose and fell in pitch as it went over. Civil War soldiers commented on the richness and variety of sounds made by shot and shell of many calibers.

The round solid shot and shell of that era made possible an extremely effective engagement technique not possible today – skipping a shot across the ground. The heavy shot could be easily seen, bouncing along the battlefield like a baseball, but

ABOVE *This photograph of a night artillery duel captures the explosions from the muzzle of the weapon and through the hole used to ignite the charge.*
BELOW *The effect of artillery fire could be devastating. This soldier appears to have been struck by a ball or shell fragment –*

his left arm has been severed and his abdominal cavity opened. A single artillery round could cut a devastating furrow through a close-packed infantry unit, chopping down one soldier after another.

even when nearly spent, the rolling solid ball of iron had enough kinetic energy to kill any man it happened to hit.

Artillery shells of that era were simple, but nevertheless sometimes quite effective. Spherical shells were simply cast-iron balls with space inside for a black powder bursting charge and a cavity for a time fuse. The ignition of the propellant charge in the gun lit the powder train in the shell's fuse; if properly cut, it would detonate the charge near the target. Generally, although not always in those primitive times, the charge would shatter the cast iron into several ragged chunks of scrap metal and propel them at high velocity in all directions.

Having an artillery round explode nearby is still an interesting experience. If you happen to be looking at the event when it occurs, you see a momentary orange flash that dissolves almost instantly into black smoke, then disappears. Some scrap iron will likely come whizzing in your direction, but bits and pieces will fall out of the sky for what seems like a long time, since some

COOLNESS IN BATTLE

Thomas Johnson served on the gun crew of a battery commanded by Captain Jenny, 3rd New York Artillery, and was wounded during action at Kinston, North Carolina. The wound was severe and Captain Jenny said to him, "Johnson, you had better to the rear and have your wound dressed."

"No, Captain," he said, "I am going to work!" He continued to serve the piece until hit again – this time by a solid shot that took off his arm. He turned to Captain Jenny and said, "Now, Captain, I guess I'll quit!"

will have been thrown up vertically and take a while to fall back to earth. It must have been like that 135 years ago, but magnified during major battles by the detonation of hundreds or thousands of projectiles.

A ROUTINE DAY IN AN ARTILLERY REGIMENT

The routine for the artillery soldier wasn't much different from that of the cavalry trooper, except that he didn't spend much time in the saddle. Day began when the bugler sounded "Reveille" at daybreak and the sergeants assembled the sleepy men for the first formation, when the roll was called. Immediately after, typically at 6 am, the bugler sounded stable call, and most of the men headed for the picket line to attend the battery's many horses. After an hour of cleaning and feeding the horses, shoveling manure, and checking the animals for injury and disease (both common), the soldiers went off to their own breakfast at the summons of the bugler at 7 am.

After breakfast, the battery often conducted drills and target practice for several hours. Then there was another formation, another roll call, and the soldiers were dismissed for lunch (called then, and now, in the US military, dinner).

More drill filled the early hours of the afternoon, from about 1 pm till 3 or 4 pm,

LEFT *Practice makes perfect. Regular drilling ensured that every man knew his role and would not be wanting in battle. This photograph of the Union Keystone Battery is by Mathew Brady (1823-96) who ruined himself financially in setting up a team of photographers to record the Civil War. His material is housed in the Library of Congress and provides a remarkable record of the conflict.*
RIGHT AND BELOW *Artillery was of particular importance in defensive positions. More Brady photographs, shows guns and other equipment captured by Grant's forces when Richmond, Virginia, fell in 1865.*

when the bugler sounded stable call again. After another hour attending to the horses, and shoveling a lot more manure, the soldiers formed up for the daily retreat formation, another roll call, an inspection, and the lowering of the flag from the camp flagpole. At 6 pm, the welcome notes of "Supper Call" drifted over the assembled multitude. Most had the next couple of hours free to smoke, play cards, talk, write letters, and read.

Some regiments and brigades with bands provided music in the evenings, and these concerts were extremely popular – when the bands were good, and some

were awful. Even when bands weren't providing entertainment, there were usually a few men in a unit who possessed musical instruments – frequently banjos and violins – and at least the fundamental skills to use them. Singing was very popular, too.

"Tattoo" was sounded at 8 pm, and "Taps" at 8:15, in some units, 9 pm in others, after which all were required to be quiet and lights extinguished.

The quality of care during stable call seems to have varied quite a bit during the months of winter, when most units stopped campaigning and tried to hibernate.

RIGHT *Union troops inspect an artillery position.*
BELOW *Another Brady photograph, this shows some of Grant's siege equipment lined up at the depot of City Point, Virginia, in 1864.*

Life in Camp and on the March

ost Civil War soldiers spent a lot of time sitting in camp, waiting for something to happen. These camps were usually laid out for regimental-sized units in a formal pattern with a parade ground, adjacent to which would be the tents of the soldiers. Behind the soldiers' tents were the tents of the sergeants, and behind them those of the officers. At the very rear of the regiment's encampment would be the tent of the commanding officer.

Both Confederate and Federal soldiers became quite skilled at turning wood lots and pastures into little cities. The site for a camp intended for a long occupation would be selected carefully. Drainage was particularly important in the soggy South, where spring and summer thunderstorms could dump several inches of rain in a

day, so the tents were always pitched on a gentle slope wherever possible.

Using the regiment's "pioneer" tools – axes and shovels – the soldiers cleared the area of trees, dug drainage ditches and a latrine for each company, called at that time a "sink."

Rather than depend on the simple and dubious protection of the Confederate- or Union-supplied tents, soldiers expecting a long stay in camp put a lot of effort into making each little abode as comfortable and homelike as possible. If planks were available, winter or summer, the tents would be pitched over wooden floors to help keep things clean. And rather than make do with the very cramped confines of the standard "dog" or "wedge" tents, the soldiers used the canvas for the roofs of more elaborate

BELOW *Getting ready for inspection. When they weren't out on the parade field practicing close-order drill and maneuvers, Civil War soldiers had to tidy up around camp, adding a bit of polish for the sergeant, but also finding time for a little goofing around.*

structures. Generally, each took the form of a little log cabin with a framework to support the canvas roof. One end contained a fireplace and chimney built of sticks, mud, and a couple of barrels scrounged from the commissary sergeant. The other incorporated the structure's front door, often no more than a piece of canvas or gutta-percha blanket tacked to the lintel.

Using no more than the abundant trees found throughout the areas in which both armies campaigned, the soldiers fashioned furniture that included bunks, tables, and chairs. When they were done with their own little homes, sometimes they fabricated large and elegant chapels in the same rustic style.

LEFT *Wedge or "A" tents were used in many variants, the worst being the simple "dog" tent, one half of which each soldier was supposed to carry in his knapsack.*

Each little cabin became home to about four men. They set up housekeeping, normally for the winter, with more comfort than would have been possible when living under canvas alone, sometimes doing their own cooking at the hearth, sometimes receiving their rations already prepared by a cook at the company cookhouse.

Life in camp, though, was not very comfortable by today's standards. The soldiers had a tremendously difficult time remaining clean, and the close confines helped spread lice, a very common problem in both armies. Everybody, from Generals Lee and Grant on down to the lowliest private, suffered from lice, and the only way to get rid of them was to boil

BELOW *Mounting guard involved a lot of the men in each unit. This is the 114th Pennsylvania Infantry headquarters guard mount, complete with white gloves.*

HOW THE VETERAN MAKES HIMSELF COMFORTABLE

Put a recruit into a forest of pine trees, with his shelter tent, and if you have nobody but recruits about him, ten to one you will find him under that shelter tent three weeks from that time.

Not so with the veteran. If he be camped in the pine forest, give him an old axe, a bootleg, a mud-puddle, a board or two, and a hand full of nails, and he builds him a house comfortable and commodious, and not wanting in architectural beauty.

First he fells his trees, then he cuts and notches his logs, and lays them together to the required height. His roof he puts on, giving it great slope, and thatching it with the green of the pine trees.

He has been careful to leave window spaces, and tacking pieces of

his shelter tent over these, he has provided light, but he keeps out the nipping air of winter. Then, with his board, he makes the door, and the bootleg supplying the hinges, it soon swings to its place.

Then he fills the spaces between the logs with soft earth from his mud-puddle, and his house is done, except the chimney, and that the forest and the mud-puddle provide, for his chimney is nothing but a pile of sticks, plentifully plastered without and within with mud.

With his old axe, he manufactures out of pine logs a full assortment of furniture – bedstead, chairs, table, wardrobe, and generally adds a mantle. Then with a bright fire upon his hearth, he is prepared to laugh at winter, and generally does.

ABOVE *Members of Company D, 22nd New York Militia, gather at their little rendezvous. The unit's housekeeping is a bit on the casual side, along with the militiamen themselves.*

LEFT *On the march, infantry soldiers who had managed to keep their gear spread their rubber sheets as protection against the damp ground and rolled into their blankets, fully clothed, for a little rest.*

ABOVE, RIGHT *Confederate soldiers built their shelters very much like their Union counterparts. These are members of the Washington Light Artillery of New Orleans, at ease before their happy home.*

the clothes and shave off all hair. Lice were such common pests that soldiers spent hours trying to dig them out of their clothes and hair, without much success. For amusement, lice were entered in races conducted in frying pans and tin plates.

There were other forms of amusement, too. Most regiments kept the men busy at drill on the parade ground every morning and afternoon, but there was plenty of time for recreation. Playing

cards was very common, with whist, euchre, and poker being quite popular, and a few soldiers won large sums of money this way.

When bored, soldiers will desperately seek out any kind of reading material, and books of almost any kind were read and re-read till they fell apart. The sutler offered cheap dime novels, some quite racy, for purchase by the soldiers. Many regiments established small camp libraries stocked with books of much higher quality, often donated by well-meaning citizens at home.

And then there was sin. Whiskey and women were popular pastimes for the Civil War soldier, Northern or Southern. Liquor was easily obtained by officers from the regimental commissary; they could buy as much as they wanted, and many of them wanted a lot. Sometimes the common soldier was permitted to purchase alcohol from the commissary, too, but only with a written authorization from his company commander, a very rare "note from mother."

Instead, the soldiers developed imaginative and effective ways to smuggle the booze in from outside camp. Friends hid bottles inside parcels and packages sent into camp, tucked them inside roast chickens, and in cans with innocent-sounding labels. They snuck in whiskey by the bottle, barrel, and case. And if it was too much trouble to bring alcohol into camp, the soldiers detoured around the pickets and sentries to go into the town or village to do their drinking.

And one way or another, soldiers will find feminine companionship, even if they have to pay for it. For many young Rebels and Yanks, going to war was their first experience away from home and the strict supervision of parents, church, and community – and they were easily tempted. While we tend to think of the Victorian age in America as being a time of extreme morality and strict social standards, it was also a time when organized and disorganized prostitution was rampant. Whenever a regiment stopped in one place for more than a few days, a platoon of women of easy virtue was likely to show up.

The soldiers were serviced in their own tents, in some units, when the commander permitted women in the company area. In fact, some commanders took up residence with prostitutes – "brevet wives" they were called, since their status was quite temporary – and lived with them in camp. Women would show up near camp and "entertain" the troops one at a time, in the woods or weeds or a house nearby.

Cities like Richmond, New Orleans, and Washington all had thriving brothel districts with dozens of whore-houses offering hundreds or thousands of prostitutes of all shapes, sizes, colors, and prices. Washington alone had about 450 brothels with around 7,500 inmates. The result, of course, was a massive epidemic of venereal disease. Approximately eight percent of soldiers, Northern and Southern, came down with one version or another of the "clap," for which at the time there was no cure.

FOOD AND COOKING

Soldiers traditionally whine and snivel about their chow, and Civil War soldiers really had something to complain about. According to regulations, the Federal and Confederate soldier should have been fat and happy, had he actually received the full daily ration to which he was due. This is what a Union soldier should have received:

• Twelve ounces of fresh pork a day, or 20 of either fresh or salt beef;
• A pound-and-a-half of flour or 12 ounces of hard bread (in camp), or 20 ounces of hard bread on the march;
• An ounce of dried vegetables;
• Plus coffee, beans, rice, sugar, salt, vinegar, soap, and candles as supplemental issue.

Few actually received their full ration, particularly when in the field, and much of the food they were given and were expected to eat was simply awful.

HARDTACK AND CORNBREAD

The foundation for the Union soldier's diet was a flat little item officially called "hard bread," but known universally as "hardtack." Made of nothing more than flour and water, without leavening, and very rarely with a little salt, then baked to the consistency of a floor tile, hardtack was what the soldier ate on the march and in camp.

Sometimes it was full of weevils and maggots, but the soldiers were expected to eat it anyway – and many of them did. Josh Billings, in his classic, *Hard Tack and Coffee* (1876), described the many ways the men in his unit tried to deal with this item of food. Gentle heating over a fire would make the weevils depart, he reported, but the maggots, if present, would stand their ground. The weevils were far more common, and Billings claimed that when consumed in the normal way (in his unit), mixed in coffee, there was no noticeable difference in flavor with or without the weevils.

The stuff was usually incredibly hard. An authentic piece of hardtack looks like a large cracker, but it is impossible to break apart with the unaided teeth of most mortals. First, it had to be broken up, usually with the butt of a musket, then the pieces were placed in the mouth or moistened in some way. After a while, they softened a bit, taking on the texture of rubber and the taste of ... well, nothing much at all. Adding them directly to coffee was, according to Billings, the standard way of making the stuff edible.

Each Federal soldier was supposed to receive nine or ten pieces of hardtack a day, a full ration being officially 12 ounces. On a forced march, there might not be anything else to eat for days at a time, and, although not very palatable or complete as a healthy diet, hardtack provided some nutrition.

When soft enough, hardtack was toasted and sometimes buttered with the rancid canned article sold by the sutler. It was crumbled and added to soups and stews as the ultimate lumpy dumpling. Some, according to Billings, tried frying it in grease, topped with a little sugar – and some soldiers would avoid eating it at all.

The South produced far more corn than wheat during the war, and instead of hardtack issued cornmeal as the foundation of the soldier's diet, or sometimes just fresh corn on the cob. Nutrition was a different problem for the Rebel soldier, and many suffered. The Confederate states produced enough for their army, but the distribution system failed the soldiers and left much of the food they might have used in decaying piles along the railroad tracks. But since the war was largely fought on Southern ground, farmers in the area of operations of Confederate units were generally more willing to support the army as an act of patriotic sacrifice – up to a point.

BEEF AND PORK

The daily meat ration, if any, was likely to be very fresh or very old. Federal infantry and artillery units brought their fresh beef with them when possible, in the form of live cattle that were driven along with the supply trains. These animals were slaughtered and butchered on the spot, chunks of fresh meat being issued to the troops almost immediately.

Since the animals were bought from the lowest bidder, they were not usually prime specimens and the meat was of indifferent quality. Each unit's ration was weighed and cut into portions to be issued to the men, sometimes individually and sometimes as units up to company size.

The ration was prepared either by unit cooks or by the men themselves.

LEFT *If the Union soldier complained about his "rusty" beef and wormy hardtack, the Confederate infantryman sometimes had to make do with fresh corn and fruit, sometimes ripe and other times not.*
ABOVE, RIGHT *A detail of soldiers cut up meat – ready for issue to the soldiers.*
RIGHT *Fresh bread issue in the field. Huge bakery operations supplied the Union soldiers near Washington, DC, and sometimes farther afield, with this comparative luxury.*

ABOVE *The conical Sibley tents in the background seemed like a good idea at the beginning of the war, but turned out to be too big and heavy to carry around during active campaigning. The wall tents in the foreground had the same problem, and were reserved for officers and hospitals.*
RIGHT *Morning and the troops are supposed to be getting ready for inspection. These Union soldiers, though, are goofing off while the sergeant is out of sight. Near Baton Rouge, Louisiana.*

Billings said that the men in his unit preferred to do their own cooking, and roasted or fried their fresh meat, given a chance. But if the unit's own cooks did the preparation, it was likely to be boiled and unappetizing.

Civil War soldiers knew better than to complain too much about the quality of the fresh pork or beef because the alternative was the salted variety, supplied to the unit in heavy brine. This process preserved the meat extremely well – almost nothing would touch it, including hungry soldiers when it was in particularly bad condition. Then, they called it "rusty," and it might be green or almost black, and smell so bad that it was inedible. Particularly loathsome salt beef would be given a very formal funeral, complete with honor guard, after which it was dumped into the slit trench latrine.

Salt pork, on the other hand, seemed to hold up a bit better. The soldiers frequently carried it on the march and ate it raw, if there wasn't a chance to cook it on the end of a stick over the coffee fire.

Fresh pork was a staple of both armies, since pigs were so common in the regions where the campaigning was done.

FORAGING

Besides the official commissary supply procedures, soldiers from both sides had another source of food and fodder of normally excellent quality, and sometimes abundance – they stole it from civilian friend and foe anywhere near the line of march.

Ducks, geese, fat cattle, pigs and piglets, turkeys, chickens, hams, barns full of hay and sacks full of oats, wheat, and barley were all fair game for the hungry soldiers, and were taken from farmers at the point of a bayonet when necessary. Sometimes the foragers would "pay" for the goods with Confederate or Union banknotes, but these could seldom be cashed in.

The rules of the game generally required that the farmer be left with just enough to get by with, and not entirely cleaned out – but that rule was not always

observed. When it wasn't, the farmer and his family sometimes starved.

BOXES FROM HOME

The commissary system provided the soldier with the basics for sustenance most of the time, but when in camp many soldiers' diets were regularly improved with supplies from home, very much as still happens today for soldiers deployed around the globe.

During the Civil War, these boxes tended to be rather sturdy wooden containers containing all sorts of items – canned meat, hams, underwear, socks, vegetables, and even cooked poultry. The postal system at the time, even with the complications of the war, must have been pretty good to get a roast chicken from home to the soldier in camp before

it came back to life in unappetizing ways, but many reports indicate this was done successfully.

Another item frequently included in the boxes, according to Josh Billings and others, was liquor. Alcohol was prohibited in camp – except for the officers, who could buy all they wanted at the commissary tent – but the soldiers seldom worried much about that regulation and imported it by any means they could. One of the ways was to get someone to pack it into a box, but this became such a common occurrence that military postal officers started opening and inspecting the the parcels. The resourceful and considerate folks from home found ways to hide the booze in tins, perhaps labeled "condensed milk."

THE SUTLER

Instead of a PX, each regiment in camp normally had its own sutler, a merchant who was authorized to set up shop near the unit. Inside the sutler's tent could be found the same basic kinds of goods stocked in any small base exchange today – soap, reading material, snack foods, replacement uniform clothing, and equipment – all at prices much higher than would be found in town. A can of condensed milk (the real article) cost $.75, according to Billings, a major expense for a private soldier earning $16 per month.

Both sides, however, got these things free when they overran an enemy camp. Then, they raided the sutler's tent and made off with anything they could carry.

ABOVE *Hard bread or hardtack was the foundation for a Union soldier's diet on the march, and sometimes in camp. Ten pieces like this were commonly issued to each soldier every day. Too hard to chew, it was commonly broken up and mixed with coffee, bacon grease, or incorporated into a soup or stew.*

LEFT *"Rusty" beef fresh from the cask is allowed to drain before being whacked into chunks for issue to the men.*

BELOW *A company commissary tent with fresh bread ready to issue. Some units had mobile ovens that followed the soldiers to the field, but many others issued raw flour, and the soldiers had to try to bake their own, sometimes wrapping dough around a ramrod and toasting it over the fire.*

SANITATION, LAUNDRY AND HYGIENE

There's an old saying that war is a dirty business, and it is true. Soldiers get dirty, and sometimes stay dirty for extended periods. Even today, a modern soldier on an operation may not be able to take off his boots for days at a time, and in heavy combat operations, like those in Vietnam or even "Desert Storm," many soldiers will not get a chance to change clothes or clean up for several days or even several weeks. During the Civil War, personal hygiene simply was not very important to many soldiers, and a lot of units, with predictable results.

Some commanders insisted on a reasonable level of personal cleanliness and even required that the soldiers bathe once a week or so, but others didn't care

and often didn't wash themselves. Some soldiers on both sides didn't remove their uniforms till they virtually fell apart after weeks or months of constant wear – they wore them all day, then slept in them at night. They were filthy, didn't care, and were not required to be any better. (Today, a man who doesn't take his personal hygiene somewhat seriously, runs the risk of being subjected to a "GI shower," when he is restrained with a blanket over his head and his comrades drag him to the shower, then use harsh soap and stiff bristle brushes to help him clean up his act.)

Even if soldiers did want to bathe, the only facility was likely to be the local stream or spring where the unit obtained its drinking water. There were no bathrooms, bath houses, or showers, in or out of camp. So the soldier who couldn't stand himself anymore had to take a dip in the creek or attempt a sponge bath, perhaps in his tent or out in the open air. It takes a brave man to strip to the skin and chip the ice off a bucket of water on a chilly December morning in Virginia, then apply this nearly freezing water (with or without soap) to his grimy hide. Sometimes the only option was, and still is, to pour a little water from a canteen onto a washcloth or small towel or directly onto the hands and wash up that way, getting at whatever parts of the body seemed most in need.

When in camp, some Civil War units had people who would do laundry for the others; sometimes this was the wife of one of the men, or it might have been one of the soldiers, or perhaps a freed black man or woman – or, in a Confederate unit, a slave. The clothes were likely to have been extremely dirty and infested with lice, and the routine way to wash them was a bit brutal – normally they were boiled in the same large kettles used by the company cooks. The boiling killed the lice and fleas in residence, but replacements seemed to appear almost immediately.

The soldier's attitude toward cleaning anything was exceptionally casual, and many didn't bother much with washing their tin plates or forks after meals. The most fastidious might rinse them off if a stream was handy, but most wouldn't

ABOVE, LEFT *Apparently the sergeant has had words with these lads – they have tidied up their uniforms and most of them look ready for inspection. Every unit, though, has a few men who wait till the last minute.*

LEFT *A Sibley tent could accommodate about 12 soldiers, but living inside one was awkward. Soldiers slept with their feet toward the center, arranged like spokes of a wheel.*

ABOVE *The cheerful chefs and KPs pause for a moment outside the cook tent before resuming work on the night's elegant and savory repast simmering over the fire.*

COLONEL ELLSWORTH'S LAST SPEECH

Commanders, during the Civil War and now, have a tradition of addressing the troops and inspiring them before battle. Here is one of those speeches, this one from the first Union officer to die in the war, Colonel Elmer Ellsworth, while at the head of his 11th New York Infantry – Ellsworth's Fire Zouaves. He spoke to them on May 24, 1861, at their retreat formation, the night before they went into action for the first time, just after the attack on Fort Sumter, when there was still hope that serious bloodshed might be averted.

Ellsworth was killed, shortly after making this address to his men while taking down the Confederate flag from the Marshall House Hotel in Alexandria, Virginia, across the Potomac River from Washington DC. Ellsworth and a squad of his Fire Zouaves pulled down the huge banner and were descending the stairs from the roof when the owner of the hotel, James Jackson, appeared with a shotgun. A scuffle ensued and Jackson got off a shot at Ellsworth, hitting him in the chest and killing him almost instantly. Corporal Francis Brownell fired his musket, hitting Jackson in the face, then ran him through with his bayonet. Ellsworth became the Union's first martyr. *The incident created an uproar; Ellsworth lay in state at the White House, and Brownell became the North's first combat hero.*

"Boys, no doubt you felt surprised on hearing my orders to be in readiness at a moment's notice, but I will explain all as far as I am allowed. Yesterday forenoon I understood that a movement was to be made against Alexandria. Of course I was on the qui vive. I went to see General Mansfield, the commander at Washington, and told him that I should consider it a personal affront if he would not allow us to have the right of the line, which is our due, as the first volunteer regiment sworn in for the war. All that I can tell you is to prepare yourselves for a nice little sail, and at the end of it, a skirmish. Go to your tents, lie down, and take your rest till two o'clock when the boat will arrive, and we will go forward to victory or death. When we reach the place of destination, act as men; do nothing to shame the regiment; show the enemy that you are men, as well as soldiers, and that you will treat them with kindness until they force you to use violence. I want to kill them with kindness. Go to your tents, and do as I tell you."

bother even then. Forks and knives were cleaned, if at all, by driving them into soft earth, rubbing any remaining food particles off in this direct, but not very sanitary, manner.

And if this sounds bad, things were actually worse. Without going too far into the details, remember that these soldiers didn't have bathrooms, or toilet paper, or any way to clean themselves most of the time. Their "sanitary facilities," at best, took the form of a straddle trench near the company area, called a "sink," a muddy, reeking version of a field latrine today – or they went out to the bushes near their tents. This latter behavior, in defiance of orders, caused General Lee to comment, "They are worse [than children] at keeping clean, for the latter may be forced."

To those soldiers, a smelly outhouse was a luxurious modern convenience. But at least that was a place where the many religious tracts and newspapers that well-meaning citizens forced upon the soldiers were really appreciated, and every one found an enthusiastic subscriber. They needed them. Because they didn't cook their food very well or at all, pork especially, or wash their food or hands, the soldiers often picked up internal parasites – tapeworm and trichinosis among many others. It is no wonder that so many soldiers were sick and so many died of disease. Although they didn't use the name at the time, nearly all these soldiers suffered from the blight and bane of dysentery – the disease that troops from World War II to the present

call the "GIs," but in those days was called the "Virginia quick-step" or the "Tennessee trot." Of the estimated 620,000 men who died on both sides during the Civil War, approximately 60 percent of them succumbed to disease.

WASHING DAY IN CAMP

"This is washing day for us," wrote a soldier of the 49th Ohio Regiment. "Washing is as much a duty as fighting. Woe to the unlucky sloven that appears at Sunday morning inspection with dirty clothes, dirty hands, long hair, or untrimmed beard. We are expected to bathe all over once or twice a week. At first, clothes washing was a tedious operation; but now there is not one of us that is not initiated into the mysteries of washing, rinsing, and wringing.

"Washing day with us has its amusements. On one occasion, last summer while we were stationed at Murfreesboro, a party of about a hundred of us were washing at a large spring on the other side of the town from where we were encamped.

"Buell's army was, at that time, exceedingly short of supplies. But few of us had more than one shirt – some were not even that fortunate. It was a warm, pleasant day. We had removed our clothes, placed them in kettles, built fires, and were boiling them out,

busying ourselves meanwhile in playing games – when, lo! a party of rebel cavalry came thundering down upon us in pursuit of a forage train that had been sent out in the morning.

"What were we to do? We had no arms with us; our clothes were in boiling hot water; the enemy were drawing near, fearfully near. Jumping over the fence, the whole party of us scud right through the town for camp like so many wild Indians, as fast as our legs would carry us.

"The citizens, supposing we would all be captured, came out in great glee, shouting, 'Run, Yanks! Run, Yanks!' as we fled through the streets. We reached camp in safety, to the great astonishment and amusement of our comrades. It was a long time before we heard the end of that washing day.

"I asked one old black woman if she didn't blush when she saw us running through town. She replied, 'Why, de Lord God A'mity bress ye, child – I couldn't blush for laughing!'"

BELOW *The one thing you can always do in camp is pose for the photographer – still a novelty in the 1860s.*

The Risk of Death In Battle

Part of the tradition of soldiering involves statistics, and those statistics normally describe events that were really awful. I served in Vietnam, for example, with a pilot who was supposed to be one of only two survivors of a Ranger company in Korea, and we young troopers were in awe of the guy. During and after the Civil War, old soldiers often claimed to be members of units that had taken tremendous losses. Their claims would have sounded something like, "My regiment marched off to war with a thousand men and thirty officers. When we mustered out in '65, only eighty-five of us were left." Well, you'd think from that claim that the rest were dead. As bad as the carnage was, no regiment suffered losses anything like that.

So, what were the chances of making it home? After the war, as a result of claims for pensions, the US government and state governments spent years trying to sort out just who served, and who survived.

The outcome was a set of very complete rosters for each Union regiment, complete with the name and disposition of each soldier – killed, missing, deserted, wounded, or mustered out at the end of the war. Confederate statistics weren't nearly so complete, but some data was available after the war.

From all of this a man named William Fox, who had heard all the claims of units being shot to pieces or entirely annihilated, made an exhaustive study of casualties during the war. The results were so surprising that they were described in the nation's most popular post-war magazine, *The Century Illustrated Monthly* (May 1888).

Fox looked primarily at battle deaths – killed in action (KIA) and died of wounds (DOW). The very worst casualties on the Union side were suffered by two heavy artillery regiments, followed by several infantry regiments.

The very worst of all US regimental casualties, in terms of the greatest

BELOW *The awful fate of war caught up with these Confederate soldiers, killed at Spotsylvania Court House and dumped in this ditch.*

number lost, were suffered by the 1st Maine Heavy Artillery, part of Birney's Division and the Second Corps. A heavy artillery regiment was almost twice the size of a standard regiment, with 1,800 men and 60 line officers (instead of the standard 1,000 men and 30 officers). During the course of the war, 1st Maine HA enrolled a total of 2,202 officers and men, and of these, 423 were killed in

LEFT *A dead soldier, still fairly fresh, lies where he fell.*
RIGHT *More dead Confederate soldiers, these gathered for burial; Spotsylvania Court House.*
BELOW *Union forces advance on the Confederate line during the Battle of New Market, which took place on May 15, 1864.*

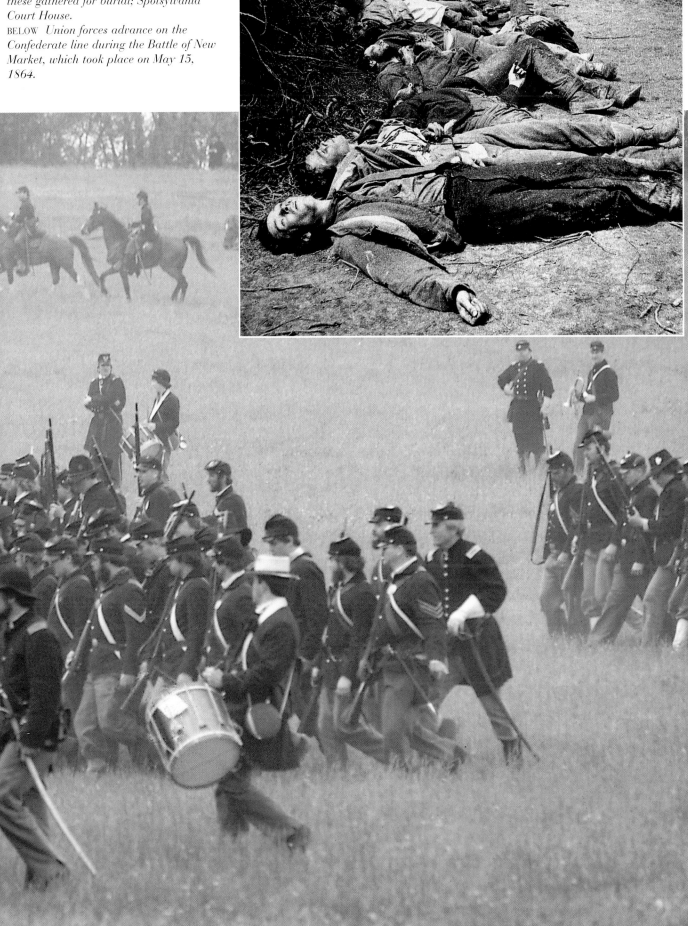

battle or died of wounds – 19.2 percent. Another 260 members of the regiment died of accidents and disease. All told, the 1st Maine HA took 1,283 killed and wounded during the course of the war, or two of every three. And about half of that number died or were wounded in just a few awful minutes during the attack on Petersburg.

The runner-up in this bloody contest for the most men lost in one regiment was another heavy artillery unit, the 8th New York. Of the unit's 2,575 officers and men, 361 were KIA or DOW, 14 percent of the total strength. The regiment lost another 302 to disease, 102 of whom died as Confederate POWs. The total of battle casualties – killed and wounded together – was 1,010, or a little under 40 percent.

Among the conventional-sized regiments, the bloodiest turned out to be the 5th New Hampshire Infantry: of the 976 names on the regiment's wartime

rolls, 295 were KIA or DOW, almost 18 percent, while another 178 died of disease.

Of the 2,000-plus regiments in the Federal force, only 35 lost more than 200 officers and men during the conflict – figures far lower than conventional wisdom suggested at the time, and quite different from the legend and lore of old soldiers.

Now, these figures are for full-up regiments over the course of the whole war. The chances of being hit were much better in some individual battles, and in some company-sized units.

For example, the 35th Massachusetts Infantry went into battle at Cold Harbor with 302 officers and men, then lost 215 – nearly three-quarters of them – killed and wounded.

And the 26th North Carolina Infantry suffered the worst losses of any regiment on either side in a single battle – 588

killed and wounded, plus another 120 missing, at Gettysburg. One company of this unlucky regiment took 100 percent casualties, each of its 84 soldiers being wounded or killed.

Another company, from the 6th Alabama, lost 21 killed and a further 23 wounded of 55 present for duty on the morning of the Battle of Fair Oaks.

LEFT *Another Mathew Brady photograph shows a Union casualty being offered water by a comrade.*
BELOW *Well-equipped soldiers were more likely to survive the rigors of war – but even then the casualties could be high. These Federals are resting after taking Petersburg, Virginia, 1865. In the assault on Petersburg on June 18, 1864, 1st Maine lost 604 men in just 20 minutes, about two-thirds of the 900 present for duty that day.*

On April 10, 1861, General P. G. T. Beauregard, provisional commander of Confederate forces at Charleston, South Carolina, demanded the surrender of the 80 Federal soldiers manning Fort Sumter, commanding the entrance to the harbor. Major Robert Anderson, commander of the garrison, refused. The Confederate batteries nearby opened fire on the fort two days later, and at 2:30 the following afternoon, unable to reply effectively, Anderson surrendered. None of the approximately 580 soldiers on both sides of the engagement was killed during the bombardment, and Anderson and his men were allowed to evacuate.

Until that moment, a war between the states had been theoretical, rhetorical, and political. After that, it became a matter of honor, loyalty, and personal integrity. During the next four years, about 2,200,000 men would serve the Union, and about 750,000 the new Confederate States

of America. Of the grand total, about 660,000 would die – most from disease, but many from a wide variety of excellent and efficient killing machines developed or employed during the conflict.

The American Civil War was a pivotal experience for individuals, for the US Army, and for the nation, which was a different kind of United States when the shooting stopped in 1865. It was a collective experience so powerful that the echoes of those guns are still heard, loud and clear, today.

They are heard especially in the ranks of today's US Army. The modern Army's foundation was laid during that war, not before. It wasn't until the Civil War that the Army really learned to fight with large units, to supply and move, and administer combat brigades, divisions, corps, and groups of corps. It wasn't until the Civil War that the Army really learned how to recruit, train, equip, and deploy hordes of

citizen-soldiers in combat, to keep them fed, supplied with ammunition, and put them and their regiments into action effectively.

Today's combat infantryman, like his Civil War ancestor, is in his late teens or early twenties, slender, and very accustomed to marching. Like his forbear of 135 years ago, he carries a rifle and bayonet, canteen, spare ammo, and a pack that weighs 50–100 pounds. His tactics are different and he is more inclined to take cover than his predecessor, but he still sleeps in the dirt, still wears his boots and uniform for days, and maybe weeks, at a time in combat, and gets just as scared and tired.

Today's soldier spends a lot of time conducting "after-action reviews" and turning the results into "lessons learned." We are still conducting after-action reviews of the Civil War, and still coming up with lessons learned.

A SOLDIER'S LAST LETTER

This letter dated July 4, 1863 was written by John Moseley, a Confederate soldier wounded at Gettysburg.

Dear Mother: I am here a prisoner of the war, and mortally wounded. I can live but a few hours, at farthest. I was shot fifty yards from the enemy's line. They have been exceedingly kind to me. I have no doubt about the final result of this battle, and hope I may live long enough to hear the shouts of victory before I die. I am very weak. Do not mourn my loss. I had hoped to have been spared, but a righteous God has ordered it otherwise, and I feel prepared to trust my case in his hands. Farewell to you all! Pray that God may receive my soul.

Your unfortunate son, John.

FAR LEFT *Success for the Union, but the detritus of war remained . . .*
LEFT, AND BELOW *Scenes around Atlanta – of the defenses (left) and of Hood's ordnance train destroyed in the retreat.*

RIGHT *The war was a long, abrasive process that ground down individuals, units, and ultimately both the Union and Confederacy.*

RIGHT *The war was a long, abrasive process that ground down individuals, units, and ultimately both the Union and Confederacy.*

THE LETTERS OF BRIGADIER GENERAL HENRY M. NAGLEE

Henry Naglee was a field-grade officer, a rank-and-file member of the general officer class. He was a West Point graduate and reasonably competent field commander, but he made one major tactical error that cut his career short – but it wasn't on the battlefield. He backed McClellan against Lincoln and was vocal in his criticism of Lincoln's administration. He was sidelined, then resigned in 1864.

Even so, these two letters to Mary Schell (an actress in San Francisco) reveal a lot about how senior officers lived in camp and in the field, and something about their attitude toward the private soldiers, too,

CAMP, 27 MILES EAST OF
RICHMOND
                    May 16th, 1862.
MY DEAREST, DEAREST PET:
I have not written for two weeks – so long, that I cannot longer be contented until I shall have done so. I have been in the last six weeks in the swamps between the York and the James rivers – not sick, not well – much sickness around us; but only too anxious to be happy with you again. I take quinine constantly, drink very little, eat nothing and that of the simplest character. Frequently I get nothing in a long march from morning until night but a hard cracker and a piece of cold pork; and frequently am out all night in the rain – without a tent, without

a blanket – standing all night – everybody under arms in his place – expecting an attack.

We have had some hard fighting. I have worked hard, but as yet not happened to be at the right spot. I made a very creditable reconnaissance on the 29th of April, in which quite a number of my people were killed. Was in the advance on Sunday preceding the battle at Williamsburg; but on Monday, Sumner and Keyes held my command in reserve all day until McClellan came up, when he sent me to support our troops that had turned the works on the left of the enemy. When I came upon the ground, the enemy gave way, and we did not get into the fight. I am happy to say to you, my own dear little one, that I have made crowds of friends with all of the promising officers, and that my command have unlimited confidence in me. We expect a hard fight at Richmond, which may come off at any moment. Gen McClellan is here, and we have a superior force of 120,000. The enemy will concentrate 170,000. But, my own dearest, darling little one, who is only so happy when nestled in the arms, upon the breast of him she loves, what do you care for all these things?

I am almost afraid to tell you, that my horse rode over one of the torpedoes that the enemy had buried in the middle of the road we had to march over to occupy their batteries at Lee's Mills, near Yorktown. It exploded immediately after I

had ridden over it, and killed and wounded seven men. The killed were mangled in the most horrible manner; their legs were torn from their bodies, and the flesh of their thighs from the bones, and the joints all separated.

The battle-field at Williamsburg was marked by a great many dead and wounded. The enemy lost about one thousand, and from what I can learn we lost not less than two thousand five hundred.

Hooker's men were slaughtered; and it is said so many more were killed, in the consequence of the confusion, by their own balls, than were killed by the enemy. I am inclined to believe the enemy got the best of it. They were inferior in numbers to us. Our men fought well. Too much censure cannot be thrown upon those in command. If McClellan had not come upon the ground, we should have been beaten – this is entre nous.

Write me a sweet, dear little letter, full of love. Tell me when you love and think of me most; tell me whether you sleep well, and whether you ever dream of me. I never hear from James, or anybody else at San Francisco, but yourself. Again, dearest angel of my devotion, upon whom I concentrate all my love, and all my desire, let us hope to be soon, very soon, happy – excessively happy together.

Your own

HARRY.